THE BODY IN ISLAMIC CULTURE

FUAD I. KHURI

THE BODY
IN
ISLAMIC CULTURE

Illustrations by Jad

Saqi Books

British Library Cataloguing-in-Publication Data
A catalogue record for this book is available from the
British Library

ISBN 0 86356 319 8 (pb)
ISBN 0 86356 974 9 (hb)

© Fuad I. Khuri, 2001
© For the illustrations, Jad, 2001

This edition first published 2001

Saqi Books
26 Westbourne Grove
London W2 5RH
www.saqibooks.com

CONTENTS

Illustrations

PREFACE

During my fieldwork in Bahrain in 1974–75, I learned that
the Shi'a hold Friday prayer provided it is led by one of three
specific *shaikhs* who were reputed to be pious and who, as it
was put to me, 'command the righteous and condemn the
forbidden'. Within a month, I arranged for an interview with
one of the *shaikhs*. Dressed in white from head to toe, he cut
an impressive figure: tall, well-built and handsome. He ushered me into his private room on the second floor of his
mansion; the first was occupied by his wives and children. It
was a very austere room with straw mats covering the floor
and scattered with old cushions, faded with repeated use.
Nothing decorated the walls, except for a Qur'anic verse:

> O ye who believe! Avoid suspicion, for suspicion
> is sometimes a sin. And spy not on each other,
> nor speak ill of each other. Would any of you like to
> eat the flesh of his dead brother.[1]

I explained to the *shaikh* the purpose of my visit – namely,
that I was interested in the organization of the Shi'a community in Bahrain and that I had some questions to ask him.
He nodded and smiled, and said in a low voice, 'I was told
you are a professor and therefore I would like to suggest that
you ask questions and I ask questions.'

I visited him several times and exchanged views and ideas

about a wide range of issues. Some of his answers were included in my book *Tribe and State in Bahrain*. His questions, however, focused on two areas: the exact dates of the death of famous Christian figures such as the Virgin Mary, Christ, John the Baptist and a multitude of saints; and female physiology and the complexity of the human reproductive system, 'the mystery of procreation', as he put it.

Our interviews went very smoothly for several weeks, and he seemed to be impressed by the knowledge I, as a Christian, had of Islam and the Qur'an. In one of these interviews, he asked:

'When did the Virgin Mary die?'

'By God, I don't know,' I answered.

'When did Christ die?' he added.

'By God, I don't know,' I replied

'When did John the Baptist die?' he inquired.

'By God, I don't know,' I responded.

Then, with some hesitation, he commented,

'Doctor, are you a Christian or a Muslim?'

'By God, I do not know,' I affirmed.

His questions about dates were understandable. The death of Imam Hussain bin Ali at the Battle of Karbala around the middle of the seventh century has been commemorated ever since in what is known as the *'Ashura* ritual. This commemoration seems to have triggered deep interest among the Shi'a Muslims in the deaths of many revered imams, prophets and saints. In fact, many books have been written about the deaths of such religious figures including the twelve Shi'a Imams and the Virgin Mary. The Shi'a hold special prayers called *qira'at* (readings) on the anniversary of these revered persons' deaths.

As for the questions on female physiology, the *shaikh*

wanted to know why women do menstruate. Why do some menstruate regularly and others irregularly? What causes pregnancy? What is 'artificial' pregnancy? What makes a woman barren? Why can some mothers breastfeed and others cannot? And many other questions of this nature. In order to answer them, I consulted a medical doctor who was a friend of mine.

In my career, I seem to have always picked up topics for research from fieldwork engagements. My interest in the body in Islam is no exception. It was initially the *shaikh*'s questioning about female physiology and the reproductive system which often touched upon the concepts of purity and pollution, that inspired me to do further research in the subject. Hence, this book on the body in Islamic culture.

Fuad I. Khuri
Reading, 12 March 2000

PART I

BODY IDEOLOGY

CHAPTER 1

Body Ideology and Body Language

This book falls in two related but different sections: the first deals with body ideology; the second with body language. In my extensive fieldwork in various Arab countries – Lebanon, Syria, Bahrain, Yemen, and Oman – I came to realize how Islam as a system of belief and law presents itself as an ideal towards which the believer must continuously aspire. The life of the Prophet Muhammad and his companions is treated as a model of behaviour to be admired and imitated. In his two books *Freedom Islam not Slavery Islam* (1979) and *Islam and the Contemporary Challenges* (1981), the late Hassan Sa'ib repeatedly makes the point that Islam is an ultimate aim whose achievement requires continuous struggle. There is faith in the struggle which makes Islam at once the goal and the means to attain it. Many Islamic jurists distinguish between the 'big struggle' and the 'small struggle'; the first refers to accomplishing the teachings of religion, the second to conquest.

The priority given to the practice of *shari'a* (religious law) in Islam, and the fact that religious law could be derived from dogma, the life of the Prophet and his companions, as well as from customary practices, affirms the belief that religious goals can be readily achieved. This is a case where ideology and behaviour are entwined, a phenomenon that can be clearly observed in the beliefs and practices related to the body.

Body symbolism in Arab-Islamic culture permeates every area of social intercourse, including faith and religion, social and cultural norms, patterns of behaviour and various modes of communication. The condition of the body reflects the depth of a person's religious faith, his status, manners, morality, up-bringing and reputation in society. Take, for example, simple body postures like standing, sitting or kneeling which express a wide range of meanings. We stand up in deference to others, especially those who are higher than us in status; to express piety in prayer, or loyalty before a martyr's tomb; to offer testimony in court or take an oath of allegiance.

Standing can express respect and deference, it can also be a form of punishment, in school, at home or in the army. The term *mawquf* (from *waqafa*: to stand up) in Arabic means detained in custody for questioning.

Standing may also be used to denote speed in performing certain acts such as saying 'he eats while standing,' meaning he is always in a hurry. 'He fucks while standing' indicates a person's capacity to dominate and/or having the ability to manipulate other people for his own interests, or that he is difficult to cheat and dupe. Arabs try to dominate their enemies or opponents by threatening to fuck their sisters or mothers even if, as often happens, by words or gestures. The term for marriage (*nikah*) in Arabic also implies intercourse. 'And marry the women of your choice;'[1] 'Men are the protectors of and providers for women.'[2] The link between the practice of sex and domination is obvious.

The meanings of body postures and gestures vary with the contexts in which they occur. For example, sitting might imply power and authority if performed within its proper framework, but it might also be insulting in certain circumstances, such as sitting down in those situations where standing expresses deference and respect. It indicates bad manners, to say the least. We sit to rest, exchange ideas, negotiate deals, or express and exercise influence and authority. Kings, queens, sultans, and emirs remain seated when they welcome guests and visitors, and where they sit represents authority. Hence, the parliament is referred to in Arabic as the seating place (*majlis*) of deputies; the cabinet, the seating place of ministers; the emir's council, the seating place of the emir – all signify power and authority.

Kneeling, on the other hand, signifies the height of glorification and praise, and appeals for compassionate understanding. We kneel in prayer before God appealing for His compassion and mercy, and before the sultan or the emir to earn his favour and avoid his fury. There is a similarity between religious symbols and the symbols of power and authority, despite their difference in meaning. Kneeling before God, for example, is worship; before man, subservience. The phrase 'we shall not kneel down', which implies struggle and steadfastness, has been repeatedly adopted as the cry of many patriotic movements and liberation fronts in the Middle East.

Much like human society, the body is divided into grades and strata beginning with the head, which represents high status, and ending with the foot, which represents low status.[3] The same principle is observed in houses, city ecology, land holdings, and in the seating order in public halls and buildings. People of high status in society live in higher houses and quarters than the commoners. They own the irrigated land near the source of water. In Ma'rib valley in Northern Yemen, the nobles own the land near the newly-built dam, and the *akhdam*, the lowest on the social scale, live and own the farthest part down the valley. Likewise, in public places and in mosques and churches, the upper classes occupy the front or higher seats and the lower classes the rear or lower seats.

Metaphorically there is an interesting correspondence between body and social gradation: those of high status are known as 'heads' (*ru'us*), 'faces' (*wujaha'*), 'eyes' (*'a'yan*), and 'bust' (*sidr*) – all refer to the upper parts of the body.[4]

Symbolically, the body is a collection of categories that convey different meanings, with its own distinct language. Blood, hair, nails, toes or fingers are not simply physical organs; they signify a complex multitude of meanings that vary according to culture and situation. Take, for example, the meanings of hair in Arab culture. Hair in bread signifies dirt; in men's moustaches, honour and manliness; in men's beards, piety. On women's faces, on the other hand, it signifies negligence.

If beards are left to grow naturally untrimmed it signifies bereavement and/or a determination for vengeance. By contrast, women in mourning traditionally cut their hair short. If men let their hair grow long, it indicates rebelliousness against the existing social and political order. This is why some dictatorial regimes in the Middle East have forbidden the young to let their hair grow long, even if it is the fashion of the day. At any rate, long hair became a fashion and symbol of youth rebellion in Europe and America in the mid-sixties.

Besides, these meanings vary with age and sex. The elderly who follow youthful fashions are dubbed *al-shaikh al-mutasabi* (the old man who pretends to be young), and women who leave the hair of their legs and face unshaven are labelled 'the sisters of men'. Except for the hair on her head, eyebrows and eyelashes, hair grown anywhere else on a woman's body is offensive. Pubic hair is problematic: men and women in the Middle East tend to shave it; in the west they tend to not to.

However, as a sign of rebellion against their traditionally oppressed status, feminists in the west often choose to let their leg hair and eyebrows grow naturally. They believe that shaving or trimming these hairs would appease men's chauvinistic tendencies and fulfil the roles men assign to women as objects of adornment. In traditional Arab culture, only women of questionable morality would leave the hair on their head loose and uncovered.

What concerns me in the coming chapters are the ideological assumptions held about the human body – assumptions that are thought to be true *sui generis* – true for the simple reason that people believe in them. These assumptions are acts of faith, ideological givens, that could not, and should not, be put to the test. In dealing with these questions and issues, I shall explore the conventionally accepted practices, what people say and do in the course of their daily interaction with each other.

In Chapter 2, I discuss interchangeability between the physical and the spiritual, i.e. how the physical, through the performance of rituals, acquires spiritual and divine values. These rituals focus on the myths of creation and on purification ceremonies – prayer, fasting, communion and rites of passage. It is through the performance of these rituals that spirituality is attained, which in turn, is expressed or communicated explicitly through physical attributes.

Chapter 3 examines body ideology and its impact on behaviour as it varies between Islam and Christianity and between men and women. Many beliefs held about men's bodies do not correspond or coincide with women's. The mere classification of 'the desire of women with heaps of silver and gold, well-bred horses, and cultivated crops'[5] shows that women are considered equivalent to these categories.

In Chapter 4, I deal with the concepts of *tahir* (spiritually pure) and *najis* (spiritually polluted) and point out that these are in the main acts of classification that do not necessarily reflect inherent qualities in creatures and things. From here on I shall use the term 'pure' and 'purity' to refer to the Arabic words *tahir* and *tahara* respectively, and the terms 'polluted' or 'pollution' to refer to the Arabic words *najis* and *najasa*.

I shall single out for discussion the widespread argument that the polluted, like pork for example, is so because it carries contagious diseases. Whether they are classified pure or polluted, all animals, including man, carry contagious diseases. I argue, following Mary Douglas, that pollution is a quality of creatures that are difficult to classify and, I might add, of behaviours that do not fit into the acceptably familiar patterns.

Purity and pollution are not static qualities; they change and contaminate other creatures and substances. Just as the polluted may cause pollution, they can be purified to generate purity. I discuss these qualities in relation to blood symbolism in Chapter 5 and semen in Chapter 6. Blood is at once pure and polluted; it radiates both purity and pollution. If blood flows naturally, it is polluted and causes pollution, but if it flows intentionally, it is pure and causes purity.

Unlike blood, semen is polluted and causes pollution irrespective of whether it flows naturally as in wet dreams or wilfully as in intercourse or masturbation. Yet, it is the source of human life. And to reconcile this dilemma many a Muslim appeals for God's forgiveness before approaching his wife.

In Chapter 7, I deal with the connection between body ideology and body language, and distinguish between language, body language and sign language. Body language often accompanies the spoken word either reproducing what is said through posture and gesture, or placing emphasis or casting doubt on the spoken word. Although linked to the spoken word, body language nevertheless has its own separate domain and standard 'idiom' that vary from culture to culture, and according to age, sex and status within the same culture.

Roughly speaking, body language can be dealt with under two subheadings: firstly, posture, where the body as a whole conveys meaningful messages; secondly, movements and gestures. The first focuses on social distance in interaction (Chapter 8) and on the strategy of sitting (Chapter 9). The second focuses on movements and gestures that signify sex (Chapter 10), fear and love, boredom and attentiveness, and a multitude of moods and personal attributes such as thrift and generosity, certainty and suspicion, strength and weakness, beauty and ugliness (Chapter 12).

In Chapter 11, I discuss what I call the 'Antara complex which refers to the belief among Arabs that love goes in one direction, like one-way traffic; it is the property of women, not men. A man falling in love is considered an act of madness – e.g. *majnun* Laila (Laila's madman) who earned this nickname because of his love for Laila. Men do not love, they make love. They love the tribe and the nation, which is an act of heroism and martyrdom. In fact, tribes and nations are metaphorically spoken of as darlings and sweethearts; the occupation of land is likened to rape. No wonder that the state of Israel is often referred to by Arabs as the 'beloved Palestine' or the 'raped land'.

While reviewing the Arabic literature on these subjects, I was bewildered by the frankness and openness in which sex and sexual problems are discussed in Islam. In the last chapter, I raise the issue of freedom of research and writing. It appears that a writer who follows Islamic dogma and addresses the Islamic *shari'a*, earns a considerable amount of freedom. Does this mean that free political action and social reform have to pass through the same channel?

CHAPTER 2

The Physical Attributes of Spirituality

The separation between body and soul, or body and spirit is repeatedly made, in one way or another, in all human societies, ancient and contemporary. Rarely do we find a society believing that the formation of flesh and blood constitutes man in his entirety, in the sense that he ceases to exist once they perish. The image of the body, its natural endowments, and its connection to the soul all vary according to religion and culture.

In this dual formation of body and soul, the body alludes to the physical, material and tangible side that withers away with time, and the soul to the eternal, everlasting part. As Abdul-Wahhab, the late famous Egyptian singer put it:

The love of the soul has no end;
The love of the body is short-lived.

The soul is the essence of things, the foundation, the base, the *raison d'être* of existence. In Arabic, we say 'the soul of roses' meaning its taste and odour; 'the soul of grapes,' its juice and wine. The soul is that part of beings and things that remains and continues after their transformation from one state to another. The soul of man survives and continues after death. Hence, the belief in reincarnation, the return of the soul to life one generation after another through a new body. Some Islamic sects, such as the Alawites and Druzes, believe that the reincarnation of souls takes place manifestly through divine intervention.

It is also possible to use the term 'soul' in Arabic to refer to the total personality. We say that a person has 'light soul', to mean that he has humour and tells jokes. In this sense, soul is used as a synonym for blood; 'light blood' and 'light soul' carry the same meaning.

These meanings of body and soul, which are taken from conventional usage, popular culture, correspond to interpretations derived from religious sources, high culture. In the Qur'an the word 'body' is used to refer to a lifeless portrait or figure as in *sura* 20:88:

> Then he brought out before them [the people] the portrait [body] of a feeble calf . . .

Or it may be used as an attribute of dead creatures as in *sura* 21:8:

> Nor did We [God] give them bodies that ate no food and were not eternal.

Likewise, in *sura* 38:34 it refers to a lifeless figure and the theme is temptation:

> And We [God] did tempt Sulaiman: We placed on his throne a body, but he turned to Us in true devotion.

However, the term *jasad* (body) is used to refer only to humans, the jinns or the angels, but not to others. This is in contrast to *jism* (mass) which refers to the collection of body organs, or to a herd of camels or other animals.[1]

On the other hand, soul as *ruh* may mean compassion as in *sura* 12:87 which states: '. . . and never give up hope of God's soul' – i.e., his compassion or mercy. It may also mean revelation or inspiration:

> And he sends down His angels with soul [inspiration] of His command to His servants as He pleases.[2]

The same meaning recurs also in *suras* 17:85 and 42:52. However, in the sense of spirit, soul refers to angels, as it occurs in *sura* 19:17:

> Then We sent to her [Virgin Mary] Our spirit [angel], and he appeared before her as a man . . .

Or in *sura* 2:87: 'We gave Jesus son of Mary clear signs and supported Him with the Holy Spirit . . .' meaning angel Jibra'il (Gabriel). It may simply refer to soul as opposed to body, 'The angels and the spirit ascend unto Him.'[3]

However, the meaning that raises questions about the overlap between body and soul or body and spirit relates to the myth of creation and unique birth – the creation of Adam and the birth of Jesus.

> When I fashioned him [Adam] and blew or breathed into him of My soul . . .[4]

> And the one who guarded her *farj* (chastity) We breathed

into her of Our spirit, and We made her and her son [Jesus] a demonstrative sign for the whole world.[5]

Clearly, the act of 'blowing' or 'breathing into' reflects the physical attributes of spirituality. The acts of 'blowing' and 'breathing into' are metaphors that signify creation by divine will. One of the requirements of marriage in Islam and Christianity is women's chastity and virginity, which suggests that the occurrence of 'blowing' and 'breathing into' with chaste (virgin) women simply reaffirms belief in virgin birth – namely, the transformation of a spiritual state into a physical form. This interpretation is reinforced by the material base of man's creation, from dust in the Bible and clay in the Qur'an.

Then the Lord God formed a man [Adam] from the dust of the ground and breathed into his nostrils the breath of life.[6]

We create man from a quintessence of clay.[7]

'Dust', 'clay', 'blowing' or 'breathing into' are all physical qualities emerging from the spirit or soul.

The interchangeability between spirit-soul and body shows that the separation between them, despite its universality, is not as distinct as the linguistic model suggests. Ideologically and behaviourally, there are many fields of interaction in which one is transformed to the other.

Nowhere does this interchangeability appear more vivid than in the concepts of purity and pollution in Islam. The purity of the body is a prerequisite for the salvation of the soul; and its pollution affirms the soul's defilement. This is the reason that Islam requires ablution before prayer. Likewise, Christianity, especially in the Eastern Orthodox Church, requires fasting before communion. Just as ablution prepares the body to receive God's compassion through prayer, so fasting prepares the faithful to accept the 'body of Christ' through communion which transforms the participants into a sacred domain.[8]

To seek purity through ablution, which involves washing different parts of the body, is not simply an act of cleanliness, it is divine cleanliness imposed by religious law. Nor is pollution simply a form of defilement; the avoidance of polluted objects is religiously sanctioned. Purity and pollution represent two ends of a continuum derived from religious texts.

The concept of purity occurs around twelve times in the Qur'an, and the concept of pollution only once. By contrast, the idea of cleanliness and dirtiness, which refer to human conditions, are never mentioned in the Holy Text. This is to be expected since religious symbols are always expressed in specialized codes. The revealed text is Qur'an, not a book; the chapter is *sura*; the sentence is verse. Likewise, poetry in the Qur'an is referred to as 'the miraculous'; law as *shari'a*; cleanliness as purity; and dirtiness as pollution.

Contextually, purity is mentioned either as a property of body conditions or a quality of divinely selected people. It occurs as a condition of menstruation:

They ask you about women's menstruation. Say: they are a hurt and a pollution. So keep away from women in their periods, and do not approach them until they are purified. Once they have purified, approach [make love to] them in the place ordained for you by God. God loves those who keep themselves pure.[9]

Or it may occur as a condition of orgasm or touching women:

> When you prepare yourselves for prayer wash your faces
> and your hands and arms to the elbows; rub your heads
> with water; and wash your feet to the ankles. If you are in
> a state of orgasm, [purify] by bathing your whole body . . .
> If you have been touching women and you find no water,
> then take clean sand or earth and rub therewith your faces
> and hands. God does not wish to place you in a diffi-
> culty.[10]

Additionally, purity is mentioned as a quality of water:

> He causes rain to descend on you from heaven to purify
> you therewith; [this is] to scrape from you the stain of
> Satan.[11]

It also occurs as a property of clothes (*sura* 74:4), or holy
scriptures (*sura* 80:13–14). It is similarly mentioned as a special quality of those who have been selected by God, such as
Issa (Jesus Christ) or Maryam (the Virgin Mary), to perform
a sacred role.

> Behold! the angels said: O Mary! God has chosen you
> and purified you – chosen you above the women of all
> nations.[12]

> Behold! God said: O Jesus! I will take you and raise you
> to myself and purify you [of the falsehoods] of the blas-
> phemous.[13]

It may also carry the meaning of making the right choice
in marriage (*sura* 2:232), or in the act of alms-giving:

Of their wealth take alms that would purify and sanctify them . . .[14]

This divine insistence on being pure is parallelled by an equal emphasis on the avoidance of pollution. Pollution is mentioned in the Qur'an in three different but related senses: *najis*, *rijs* and *rijz*. This, by itself, shows how meticulous Islam is about the concepts of purity and pollution.

In the sense of *najis*, pollution occurs only once in the Qur'an regarding the entrance of the polytheist to the Sacred Mosque:

O ye who believe! Truly the polytheists are polluted (*najis*), so let them not approach the Sacred Mosque . . .[15]

However, other words, like *rijs* and *rijz*, that carry more or less the same meaning as *najis*, occur more frequently. *Rijs* occurs about ten times in reference to the avoidance of forbidden acts or things including wine, gambling, divination tools (*sura* 5:93) or dead meat, running blood and pork.

Say! I find not in the Message received by me by inspiration any food forbidden unless it be dead meat, blood poured forth, the flesh of pigs, or meat prepared for deities other than God[16] – these are *rijs*.[17]

It also refers to evil or disgraceful acts (*sura* 333:33), pain and suffering (*sura* 6:125) or doubt and suspicion in the teaching of Islam.

But those in whose hearts is a disease – it will add doubt (*rijs*) to their doubt, and they will die as infidels.[18]

Thus does God make *rijs* (penalty) on those who do not believe.[19]

Like *rijs*, *rijz* refers to forbidden and filthy acts, as in *sura* 74:5, or more often to diseases, catastrophes, suffering or pain.[20]

The meanings of these three concepts (*najis*, *rijs* and *rijz*) overlap. Ibn Manzur, the famous Arab linguist, does not differentiate between them. He says: 'They all refer to the forbidden, the filthy, the blasphemous, the bad deeds; the suffering, the painful, the doubtful, and the plague.'[21] Upon closer scrutiny, although these terms seem to overlap in meaning, they may differ in their source. If Satan is the source of these abominations, then they are referred to as *rijs*; but if the source is God, they are called *rijz*, a form of punishment for disobeying divine law.

However different, these concepts signify varying scales of physical condition which, in turn, mark particular spiritual or religious achievements. In one of my interviews with a high-ranking jurist, I asked: 'My *shaikh*! Why is it that your clothes are always impeccably clean, fingernails well polished, beard well trimmed, teeth well kept; and you are always in good humour, cool and calm?'

He answered: 'This is a gift from God. Spirituality cannot be attained with a filthy appearance.'

This explains why the *ulama* class in Islam take meticulous care of their appearances. Cleanliness and decorum express purity, and purity is an act of faith. In brief, the purity of the soul is derived from physical purity which, if defiled, must be purified by 'absolute water': 'We send down from the skies water that purifies.'[22]

'Absolute water' is what nature delivers: rainfall, springs, floods, melting snow, running water, or mineral water. Other forms of water, called 'modified waters', are those that change colour, taste or odour. They are considered unclean and therefore unfit for ablution or other purification purposes. However, should defiled objects fall in absolute water they remain pure provided they do not change colour, taste, or odour. Other liquids such as tea, coffee, vinegar, rose water, juices, and the like, which are referred to in the literature as 'adjoined waters', are pure but do not purify.[23]

The polluted can be purified only by the use of absolute water, or by sand or soil (*sura* 5:7). According to Islamic *shari'a*, washing for purification should be carried out after reaching orgasm through intercourse, masturbation or wet dreams; after menstruation and parturition; after death or touching the dead. In other situations such as touching dogs or pigs, or any other polluted objects, washing is commended, but not compulsory.

At this point, we should raise the question: how are physical conditions transformed into spiritual realities? The answer lies in the practice of a multitude of rituals ranging from rites of passage, as practised in many primitive societies, to the holy mass in Christianity and the intensive performance of prayer and purification rituals in Islam. To illustrate the point, however, I shall confine myself here to a brief comparison between Islam and Christianity.

In general, Islam requires the faithful to pray five times a day, and every prayer is preceded by ablution which entails washing the face, the hands and the feet. The body should also be purified whenever it comes in contact with pollutants either through secretions – urine, semen, solid waste, menstrual blood, and the like; or by contagion, such as touching the dead, dogs or pigs. Obviously, the intensity of prayer and the purification rituals that follow continuously urge the faithful to seek personal spiritual fulfilment.

This ritualistic approach to spirituality is reinforced by the popular usage of interjections that invoke God's name and which punctuate all sorts of actions and exchanges. These include *ya-llah, wa-llah, ba-llah, insha-llah, alla-hu akbar, astaghfiru-llah* and *ma-sha'a-llah.*

Ya-llah, meaning 'oh God,' is used to mean 'hurry up', 'let's go', 'come along', 'all right' and the like. *Wa-llah* and *ba-llah* are forms of swearing, which literally mean 'by God,' used emphatically to stress a point, cast doubt, or express surprise or admiration. *Insha-llah* (if God so wishes), which is one of the first useful phrases foreigners visiting Arab countries learn, is used to affirm a commitment, accept an invitation, or appeal to God's support; or contradictorily be evasive, delay action, show indifference, or decline an invitation.

Alla-hu akbar (God is greater), which is formally used as a call for prayer, can likewise be used as a war cry, or to initiate a fight or put an end to it. It can also denote agreement or disagreement with a point under discussion; enchantment or disenchantment with an action; belief and disbelief. Consider the following anecdote about Makram Ubaid, the late Christian Copt who was appointed minister in Nahhass Pasha's government which came to power in Egypt immediately after independence. Following a heated argument with the Prime Minister, Ubaid muttered in disapproval: '*Alla-hu akbar, alla-hu akbar*'. The Prime Minister turned to him and said, 'Are you converting to Islam, Makram?' Ubaid then responded, 'My lord, it is said for blasphemy!'

Likewise, the expression *astaghfiru-llah* (I submit to God's forgiveness) is uttered at every instance of bad behaviour or ill-mannered conduct. And since Islam is a comprehensive religion in the sense that it offers the faithful an answer to every question, this may cover the entirety of man's actions or interactions. In brief, the faithful are in constant search for spirituality through rituals of physical purification and/or continuous invocation of God's name.

What is achieved in Islam by purification rituals and continuous spontaneous appeals to God is achieved in Christianity by communion. According to the Eastern Orthodox Church, for example, the Holy Liturgy passes through three stages. The first engages mainly the priest who privately prepares the transformation of bread and wine into the body of Christ. The second, which is dominated by appeals to God, tries to establish social solidarity uniting the various parts of the church community. Here, by repeatedly appealing to God to be merciful and forgiving, the social limits of the church community are defined.

Once this is done, the third stage ensues whereby the whole congregation enjoys divine, spiritual communion, in the sacramental partaking of the Body of Christ.[24] Indeed, the holy liturgy focuses in its entirety on the miraculous birth, death and then resurrection of Jesus. Through these rituals the Body of Christ is consumed and consequently the congregation is transformed into a divinely united church.

The embodiment of spirituality is perhaps nowhere more evident than in Sufi practices. The Sufis lead a very austere life in the hope that self-denial will prepare the body to be occupied by divinity, thus achieving a state of perfection. In a state of perfection, Islamic laws that are made essentially to organize physical desires will be neutralized; bodies thus prepared to receive divinity become self-regulatory. They do not need laws because they become sinless.

Many rituals that transform physical conditions into spiritual realities and vice versa concentrate on rites of passage – namely, birth, death, and adulthood.[25] These stages of growth are always accompanied by physical transformation, which suggest that the accompanying rites and rituals have been, in the main, occasioned by physical conditions.

In brief, the separation between body and soul, or body and spirit, must not be construed to mean that the two are mutually exclusive and independent. They overlap and interlock. Just as physical conditions may express spiritual moods, spiritual attainments require physical transformations.

CHAPTER 3

The Human Body: A Religious View

In the preceding discussion, I showed how physical conditions affect spirituality in such a way that the separation between body and soul, or body and spirit, becomes redundant. Through a variety of rituals, one is thereupon transformed to become the other. In the following two chapters, I shall deal with a different but related issue – namely, how body ideology affects behaviour and the day-to-day interaction between people. I shall also compare Islamic and Christian views.

In Islam, the human body is a source of shame and therefore it should be concealed and covered. This sense of shame goes back to Adam and Eve, when, upon the insistence of Satan, they tasted of the tree of life. *Sura* 7:22 states:

> So by deceit he [Satan] brought about their [Adam and Eve] fall [from paradise]: when they tasted of the tree their shamefulness [nakedness] became manifest to them, and they began to sew together the leaves of the Garden over their bodies.

Obviously, Adam and Eve became aware of the shamefulness of their naked bodies after they had fallen victim to
Satan's temptation. The body as a source of shame applies
to both men and women alike.[1] Though in varying degrees,
both are urged to be modest, keep clean and protect their
chastity. Apart from veiling, women's traditional costume is
strikingly similar to men's: long dresses that cover the body
from the neck to the feet, coupled by a head-scarf covering
the entire head except for the face. When the face is covered,
as in veiling, no part of the body, with the exception of the
eyes, is exposed:

> Say to the believing men that they should lower their gaze
> and fortress their *farj* (nakedness, genitalia); that will be
> more fitting of them. And God is well acquainted with
> all that they do.[2]

> And say to the believing women that they should lower
> their gaze and fortress their *farj*; that they should not dis-
> play their beauty and ornaments except what [ordinarily]
> appear thereof.[3]

> For men and women who fortress their *farj* [who guard
> their chastity]. For them God has prepared forgiveness
> and great reward in the afterlife.[4]

To 'lower the gaze', which literally means not to stare at people or look them in the eye, i.e., to look sideways or
downward, signifies politeness and humbleness. Many western expatriates working in Arab countries have seen this
custom as limiting social intercourse, especially if pratised
between men and women. Likewise, to 'fortress their *farj*' is

to be clean, modest and chaste. With regard to women, it implies preserving virginity, 'drawing their veils over their bosoms' and refraining from 'tapping the floor to draw attention to their hidden ornaments' (*sura* 24:31).

I am using the words genitalia and nakedness to stand for the Arabic word *farj*. There is no word for *farj* in English; it is a clear case of polysemy, a word carrying many meanings. It may be used to refer to that part of the human body that lies between the legs (genitalia), or between the navel and the knee, or between the hands and the legs.[5] In other words, it may indicate the whole naked body or part of it depending upon the context in which it occurs. As a matter of fact, every time *farj* is mentioned in the Qur'an, it is always preceded by the qualifying verbs to guard, to fortress and to protect.[6] According to Ibn Mandhur, *farj* may also mean embellishment, clothes or naked appearances – in all these cases it is a source of shame.[7]

These words – *farj*, body, genitalia, nakedness, embellishment, shamefulness – are metonyms that carry behaviourally and symbolically the same meaning and are subject to guarding and protection.[8] Much like *farj*, embellishment should be guarded and protected, as cited in *sura* 24:31.

And say to the believing women that they should lower their gaze and guard their *farj*. They should not display their ornaments . . .

The verse then defines the kin and other people to whom women may expose their ornaments; these include:

Husbands, parents, husbands' parents, children, grandchildren, husbands' children, brothers, brothers' children, sisters, and sisters' children or their wives, the slaves, the male servants, or young children who have no shame of sex yet.[9]

Interestingly, this set of kin corresponds to the incest group whom a person is not allowed to marry and who do not present a sexual threat.

Men are not exempt from the rules of modesty; they should not expose their naked bodies even to their closest relatives. Visitors are requested not to enter a house before asking permission, especially at dawn, noon or at dusk, the times of day Muslim believers may be undressing for purification purposes before prayer.[10] In my fieldwork in Bahrain I was told that fishermen are the lowest on the social scale because they expose their bodies. Even wearing short trousers in the heat of summer is considered abhorrent behaviour in traditional Muslim communities.

In brief, the human body is a source of shame that must be concealed and guarded. Among the rules of guarding the *farj* for women is to remain at home and refrain from displaying 'dazzling' looks. It is cited in *sura* 33:33:

> And stay quietly in your [the Prophet's womenfolk] houses and make not dazzling displays like the former times of ignorance . . .

The Qur'an warns women not to be seduced by the words of men with 'disease' in their hearts. Obviously, disease in this context refers to sexual desire.

> O women of the Prophet! You are not like other women. If you have piety, don't be taken by honeyed words, lest

the one who has disease in his heart be encouraged [to approach you].[11]

Exposing one's ornaments to the public, displaying 'dazzling' looks or exhibiting the *farj* generate impurity, and therefore must be avoided (*sura* 33:32–33). Guarding the *farj* in Islam is parallel to humbleness, truthfulness, patience, piety, alms-giving, fasting, and repeatedly and regularly invoking the name of God.

For Muslim men and Muslim women, for believing men and believing women, for devout men and devout women, for men and women who speak the truth, who have patience, who humble themselves, who give alms to the poor, who fast, who guard and fortress their *farj*, and for men and women who continuously remember God, for them God has prepared forgiveness and great reward in the afterlife.[12]

The mere fact that guarding the *farj* is classified along with all these religiously sanctioned forms of conduct suggests that it is equivalent to them in value. Like fasting and alms-giving, to mention only two qualities, it enables the believers to earn God's forgiveness and divine rewards.

Much of the details about guarding and protecting the *farj*, veiling, staying at home, not being seduced by honeyed words, avoiding 'dazzling' looks or tapping the floor to attract attention, and other practices that relate to chaste and modest behaviour, seem to concern women more than men. With regard to men, the directives seem to be general – i.e., to guard their *farj* without a detailed description of how it should be done. Indeed, much of the rules about men's chas-

tity or modesty is derived from the life of the Prophet and
his companions, who present themselves as models to be
imitated.

This discrepancy between men and women suggests that
women's bodies do not correspond to men's, even though
they were considered to be created from the same source:

> O people! Revere your God who created you from a sin-
> gle soul, and created from [it] her mate, and from the
> twin an abundance of men and women.[13]

Although men and women are equal in the act of creation,
their bodies are not the same. The Qur'an draws a portrait
of the female body and the way it should be treated as if it
were one of the pleasures of this world's life. In this sense, as
an item of pleasure, the female body is equivalent to having
an abundance of children, tons of gold and silver, well-bred
horses, herds of domesticated animals, and cultivated land.

> It was adorned for people the love of the desire of women,
> sons [children], tons of gold and silver, branded horses,
> herds of domesticated animals, cultivated land. Such are
> the possessions [pleasures] of this world's life.[14]

If the love of women is an item of this world's pleasures or
possessions, approaching or touching them is contradictorily a source of defilement that should be purified before
prayer.

> O ye who believe! don't approach prayer if you . . . had
> orgasm . . . until you bathe. And if you were sick or on a
> journey, or returning from the toilet, or ye have been in

contact with women, and ye have found no water cleanse yourselves with sand and earth.[15]

Therefore, intercourse or even touching women, like sickness and travel, generates a polluted state to be purified before prayer. The discrepancy between men's and women's bodies becomes more apparent in the conditions Islam stipulates for prayer, which includes, among other things, a state of purity, clarity of intent, facing Mecca, and covering the body. These conditions are equally required from men and women; the difference lies in what constitutes shamefulness for men as opposed to women. While men's source of shamefulness refers to that part of the body that lies between the navel and the knee, women's shamefulness refers to the whole body.[16] The body is a source of shame and its secretions – urine, blood, semen, infected blood, and vomit, are all pollutants that need to be purified before prayer.

There is also an injunction against painting or drawing the body. Perhaps, it is this image of the body that made Islamic art focus on calligraphy and arabesque designs rather than on human forms and looks, however charming. In those instances of modern Islamic art where the body forms the central theme, the stress is placed upon its expressive value, the symbolic meanings rather than its detailed anatomy.

These ideological images of the human body in Islam do not, in any way, correspond to its understanding in Christianity. The difference can at once be grasped if we compare the general internal layout of the church and the mosque. As we enter a mosque, we see no image of any kind; no painting, sculpture, icon or drawing resembling the human body. To have a human image of any kind is considered an act of blasphemy and polytheism. However, the absence of human motifs must not be construed to mean that mosques are always left undecorated. On the contrary, they are decorated, but with calligraphy, colour, and arabesque designs, which do not represent life. Only God is the Living, Self-subsisting and Eternal.

By contrast, as we enter a church, the Eastern Orthodox Church for example, we are immediately faced with icons of saints and angels decorating the partition hiding the altar (the iconostatis) in the front and the church walls on the sides. The icons of Christ and the Virgin Mary, the largest of them all, are placed respectively on the right and left side of the altar's entrance. We often see the portrait of Christ in human form, half naked, crucified, with a thorny wreath on his head; blood dripping from the head, the hands, and the feet where his body is nailed to the cross. His crucified body, the thorny wreath, and the spilling of blood stand for the suffering of Christ, which the Christians believe is the way to human salvation.

However, Christian churches differ in depicting the suffering of Christ and other religious images. Whereas the Orthodox Church, for example, uses the icon, which is a two-dimensional representation of reality, to underscore the symbolic meaning of the image, the Catholic Church manipulates the three-dimensional form in statues, paintings and drawings. The Protestants, on the other hand, avoid the use of artistic images altogether, while the Anglicans might paint the windows of their churches with icons and decorate the corners with statues, but for sheer decorative purposes that carry no particular religious meaning.

Like the Holy Liturgy, Christian art focuses on the birth, death and resurrection of Christ and on the miracles he performed. In these events – birth, death and resurrection, the body takes on a very peculiar religious meaning. In Christianity, the human body is made divine through the embodiment of Christ, which means that God has taken on a human shape. This is why, according to the Orthodox Church, man's salvation could be attained in body and soul. As Ware, quoting John the Damascene, puts it, 'The word made flesh has deified the flesh.'[17] Likewise, it is cited in the Gospel according to Luke: 'And all mankind shall see God's deliverance.'[18]

The emphasis Christians place on the divinity of the body led to an equal emphasis on its salvation, thus placing true faith, the acceptance of Christ, in the heart, which blends together faith and feelings, thought and will. Here the emphasis is placed on man as a whole.[19]

The divinity of the human body can be traced back to the theory of creation.

Then God said, Let Us make man in Our image and likeness to rule over the fish in the sea, the birds of heaven, the cattle, all wild animals on earth . . . So God created man in his own image; in the image of God he created him; male and female he created them.[20]

To say that God created man in his own image does not mean, as the Orthodox Church has it, that God has a body and that this body takes on a human shape; to insist on this interpretation is blasphemous. The Orthodox fathers believed that God appeared in the shape of a human body, but that God himself has no image. He is a Holy Trinity, simultaneously the Father, the Son and the Holy Spirit. Because of the Trinity composition, God spoke in the plural form: 'let Us', 'Our image', 'Our likeness'. Within the Trinity, it is the Father who represents the Kingdom of God. According to the symbol of faith, the Creed, Christians pray as follows:

> I believe in one God, creator of heaven and earth and of all things visible and invisible . . .[21]

As Ware puts it: 'God is one essence in three persons.'[22] However, this Orthodox interpretation of the Trinity which gives priority to God, the Father, from whom both the Son and the Holy Spirit had emerged, is not universally accepted in the Christian world. The Catholic Church, for example, places emphasis on the essential equality between the three components of the Trinity.

Many of the Orthodox fathers, such as John the Damascene, distinguish between image and likeness, on the grounds that image, which means icon in Greek, is a natural endowment of man, bestowed upon him by the act of creation. Man inherits the image which sets him apart from other creatures by birth. By contrast, the likeness is a moral achievement acquired by man through his deeds and behaviour, and the way he approaches God.[23] It is through the likeness of God, not the image, that man becomes capable of joining God.

Both Muslims and Christians agree that the image of man is God's creation. The Qur'an states:

> We created you and gave you shape [image] and then said to the angels bow down to Adam . . .[24]

> And God gave you shape, and made it fine, and to him is the final destiny.[25]

In the Qur'an, God created man and gave him the finest shape; in the Bible, God created man and gave him His image. Ultimately, the finest shape could only correspond to God's image.

Man in Christianity is an extension of God on earth. It is cited in the Bible:

> This is my sentence: Gods you may be, sons all of you of a high god, yet ye shall die like men die; princes fall, every one of them, and so shall you.[26]

When the Jews challenged his claim of being the son of God, the Messiah, Jesus answered, 'Is it not written in your own law, I said, you are Gods?'[27] In Christianity, there is a linkage between God and man in the act of creation; they are the sons of the High God. On this basis, it is possible for man to join God through communion symbolically turning the church into the body of Christ.

The embodiment of the Lord in the son – Jesus Christ, has transformed the human body from a physical status into a spiritual reality. Consequently, the body could not, any more, subsist on food alone. In his first letter to the Corinthians Paul writes:

> Food is for the belly and the belly for food. True, one day God will put an end to both. But, it is not true that the body is for lust; it is for the Lord, and the Lord for the body.[28]

To say 'the Lord for the body' transformed the body into an object of salvation and a feature of eternity: 'The fornicator

sins against his own body.'[29] Thus, caring for the body became a religious duty, a pillar of faith, and an act of worship.

> Do you not know that your body is a shrine of the ind-
> welling Holy Spirit, and the spirit of God's gift to you?
> You do not belong to yourselves; you were bought at a
> price. Then honour God in your body.[30]

These succeeding texts from the Bible: 'the body for the
Lord and the Lord for the body,' 'the fornicator sins against
his own body,' 'your body is a shrine of the indwelling Holy
Spirit' make it clear that the body in Christianity refers to
the entire existence of man, his whole personality and destiny. Hence, the belief that marriage unites husband and wife
in one body, one being with a single destiny.

> You surely know that anyone who links [in marriage] him-
> self with a harlot becomes physically one with her, for
> the Scripture says, the pair shall become one flesh; but he
> who links himself with Christ is one with him, spiritu-
> ally.[31]

The act of 'becoming' in the last text shows that the body
is not a fixed, static reality; it is a changing phenomenon. It
changes either through marriage or faith, or through the two
together. Consider the following passage:

> If a Christian has a heathen wife, and she is willing to
> live with him, he must not divorce her; and a woman who
> has a heathen husband willing to live with her must not
> divorce her husband. For the heathen husband now be-
> longs to God through his Christian wife, and heathen wife

through her Christian husband. Otherwise your children would not belong to God, whereas in fact they do.[32]

Through marriage, the unity of two bodies in one, holiness could be transferred from the faithful to the heathen. The sanctity of the body is a transferable commodity. No wonder that the church, the Orthodox Church for example, considers marriage one of the seven sacraments of religion; the others being priesthood, baptism, repentance (confession), grace, ointment and the sacred oil. Each of these sacraments is capable of transferring holiness from one person, place, or thing to another. It is, perhaps, because of this capacity that they are regarded as sacraments.

Just as the body in Christianity is capable of being transformed, it is equally capable of transforming things; it is at once the subject and the object combined. This capacity takes place through communion, the ritualistic consumption of the Body of Christ, 'the bread of life'. Christ says:

> I am the bread of life. I am speaking of the bread that comes from heaven, which a man may eat, and never die. The bread which I will give is my own flesh; I give it for the life of the world. Whoever eats my flesh and drinks my blood dwells continually in me and I dwell in him.[33]

The body itself is a symbol. In Christ's words, 'Whoever eats my flesh and drinks my blood dwells continually in me and I dwell in him,' 'body' signifies faith and belief, and 'eating' stands for membership in the holy community, the church. And this is in fact what Christians do in every mass through communion, where bread symbolizes Christ's flesh and wine his blood.[34] Hence the phrase, 'the church is the body of Christ,' as evidenced in the first letter of Paul to the Corinthians: 'Do you not know that your bodies are limbs and organs of Christ.'[35]

It is worth mentioning at this stage that seeking affinity to a community through partaking of the sacrificial meal is an old religious tradition practised by the ancient Semites. Because the Semites were the first in history to do this, Robertson Smith considers it the earliest form of collective worship, and therefore the origin of religion,[36] the Semitic religions: Judaism, Christianity and Islam.

Paul's affirmation, 'Your bodies are limbs and organs of Christ' places emphasis on the element of performance, the coordination between the various parts of the body. In other words, the church, like Christ's body, is composed of different but related parts each of which reinforces the functions of the others. How true in theory, and not in practice. Since its inception the church has witnessed severe schisms and internal strife.

CHAPTER 4

The Pure and the Polluted

How the human body is viewed ideologically has a considerable impact upon behaviour and interaction. If the body is a source of shame and impurities, it should then be covered, concealed and continuously purified. By contrast, if it is divine, capable of being saved, if it is 'the shrine of the indwelling Holy Spirit', and if 'God [is] for the body and the body for God', then the body is *ipso facto* pure. In Christianity, the human body is pure simply because it is an extension of God on earth. Purity is not confined to man; it is likewise extended to all creatures. All are created by God and what God has created cannot be contaminated by man. It is cited in Acts of the Apostles:

> Next day, while they were still on their way and approaching the city, about noon Peter went up on the roof to pray. He grew hungry and wanted something to eat. While they were getting it ready, he fell into a trance. He saw a rift in the sky, and a thing coming down that looked like a great sheet of sail-cloth. It was slung by the four corners, and was being lowered to the ground. In it he saw creatures of every kind, whatever walks or crawls or flies. Then there was a voice which said to him, 'Up Peter, kill and eat.'

But Peter said, 'No, Lord, no, I have never eaten anything profane or unclean.' The voice came again a second time: 'It is not for you to call profane what God counts clean.'[1]

Thus, impurity or pollution, as an inherent quality of creatures and things, has been wiped out for ever. No food is believed to be impure. In his letter to the Romans, Paul states:

I am absolutely convinced, as a Christian, that nothing is impure in itself; only if a man considers a particular thing impure, then to him it is impure. If your brother is outraged by what you eat, then your conduct is no longer guided by love. Do not by your eating bring disaster to a man for whom Christ died . . . the Kingdom of God is not eating and drinking, but justice, peace, and joy, inspired by the Holy Spirit.[2]

It can be deduced from the preceding passages that Christianity has removed the quality of impurity from the natural world, including man, and placed it in human society. 'Nothing is impure in itself,' impurity is to eat something that might outrage a brother. This interpretation is reinforced by the following passages taken from Mark:

Do you not see that nothing that goes from outside into a man can defile him, because it does not enter into his heart but into his stomach, and so passes on into the drain. Thus he declared all foods clean. It is what comes out of a man that defiles him. For from inside, out of a man's heart, come evil thoughts, acts of fornication, of theft, murder, adultery, ruthless greed, and malice; fraud, indecency, envy, slander, arrogance, and folly; these evil things all come from inside, and they defile a man.[3]

The Christian understanding of impurity, pollution or defilement, which focuses on the quality of life in a human society and the type of relationships that prevail thereupon, has drastically modified the Judaic beliefs that creatures and things are classified into pure and polluted on the basis of their genetic endowment. In Christianity, the notion of impurity and pollution has taken on the meaning of evil deeds, and as such it is confined only to human actions. The phrase 'men with impure souls' refers mainly to evil deeds or ideas.[4]

Therefore, Christ's words: 'Do not suppose that I have come to abolish the law and the prophets; I did not come to abolish, but to complete,'[5] must be reconsidered. With regard to the notions of purity and pollution, Christianity rejected the tenets of the Talmud and the teachings of the prophets. The word 'complete' could be used in two different senses, to seek perfection or continuation. Regarding the pure and the polluted, Christ's words were not meant to continue the Talmudic tradition which he managed to reject, but to seek perfection.

Unlike Christianity, Islam, which appears to have adopted the Judaic tradition, submits that creatures and things are inherently pure or polluted by virtue of their own constitution. Consequently, the whole world – man, animals, birds, fish and whatever foods are derived from them – is divided into sets and categories classified as either pure or polluted. The animals with split hooves that chew the cud such as cattle, buffalo, sheep and goats are classified in the pure category and therefore edible; the animals with claws, canines such as lions, tigers, leopards, cats, and dogs are classified in the polluted category and therefore forbidden.[6]

Except for some scattered instances, e.g. camel meat, the Islamic classification system of foods corresponds to the Jewish system. In Judaism (Leviticus 11:4–5), camels are classified in the unclean category because they do not have cloven hooves; in Islam, camel meat is clean and edible. Likewise, while horse, mule or donkey meats are forbidden in Judaism, they are reluctantly permissible in Islam out of dire necessity.[7]

In Islam, the following categories are considered unclean and therefore inedible: the dog and the pig; the elephant, the bear and the bat; predatory birds that have paws such as the eagle, the hawk, the crow. Concerning insects, Islamic jurists, for lack of a clear text, permit the beneficial and ban the harmful following the verse, 'He commands them for what is beneficial and forbids them from what is harmful.'[8] Of creatures that live in water, fish having no fins or scales are forbidden,[9] much like Jewish law in the Old Testament.[10]

What applies to land animals, birds, and fish applies likewise to the foods derived from them – namely, milk and eggs. If the meat is forbidden, milk and eggs become equally nonpermissible, and vice versa.[11] Excepted from this ruling is 'running blood' which is textually forbidden.[12]

The question is: why are certain categories classified polluted and therefore forbidden while others are pure and therefore edible? Put differently, why is goat, sheep and cattle meat permissible, whereas pig, dog, cat, snake, or rabbit meat forbidden?

Many of the Islamic jurists and some of the faithful try to explain the 'forbidden inventory' on one of two grounds, either that the categories with canines, claws and paws are carnivorous and predatory or medically harmful in the sense that they cause or carry contagious diseases.[13] To begin with, not all animals with canines and claws are carnivorous e.g. the elephant has canines but subsists on vegetables; the rabbit has claws but feeds on plants. They maintain, moreover, that the rabbit is forbidden because it menstruates like human females,[14] and menstruation is a pollutant. In fact, all mammals that lactate menstruate.

It is also believed that the pig is forbidden because it is unclean, loves garbage and subsists on dirt, and that its fatty meat is harmful especially to people who live in hot climates. The same thing can be said about chicken which loves garbage and eats human waste. In Lebanon, locally produced eggs laid by free-range hens that feed on dirt, are twice as expensive as farm eggs. And roast chicken is the pride of the elite's cuisine.

Besides, there is no animal or bird which is free of diseases that can be transmitted, in one way or another, to man. Because of their frequent occurrence, these diseases are collectively known as 'zoonosis'. These include chicken pox, anthrax and tuberculosis which has afflicted man since ancient times; they have been diagnosed in Egyptian mummies. Chicken pox could be transmitted to man from cattle, sheep, goats, pigs, or chicken; tuberculosis from mainly cattle and pigs; anthrax from sheep. There is also rabies, which is transmitted to man and other mammals from dogs; scrapie from sheep; salmonellosis from chicken, ducks, geese, or turkeys; BSE, 'mad cow disease', is the most recent discovery and is transmitted from cows.[15]

Clearly, the medical argument does not answer the question why some animals are classified pure, and some polluted. Why animals with canines and paws, and birds with claws are considered polluted; their meat forbidden? What is wrong with animals having canines and paws, and birds having claws? Put differently, what is right in animals that chew the cud and have cloven hooves, or fish having fins and scales?

Part of the answer may simply lie in the ability of man to

domesticate the animals that feed on grass, chew the cud and have cloven hooves; these are collectively referred to in the Qur'an as 'the soft animals' (an'am). Other species with canines, claws and paws were not easy to domesticate and ancient man did not have the tools to overpower them; thus they lay outside his immediate environment, the animal species he controlled. However, this simple explanation does not apply to the pig, the dog, the rabbit and other animals and birds that are forbidden but can be easily overpowered. Although polluted, these animals and birds have been domesticated and therefore lie within man's immediate domain.

Of the polluted species that lie within man's domain, the pig and the dog seem to have received considerable attention in Islamic treatises. There is hardly a jurist of consequence in Islam who fails to address this problem. The reason is not difficult to find. The concern with the pig might be traced to the fact that it constitutes an essential part of the diet of many cultures neighbouring Islam, in Europe and South Asia for example, plus the fact that many Muslim societies such as Malaysia and Bosnia eat pig meat.

The dog, on the other hand, is one of the first animals domesticated by man. Many people keep dogs which are known for their trustworthiness and serviceability. It is a multi-purpose animal. It is used in hunting, guarding, grazing sheep and goats, police work, finding survivors after a disastrous event and, most important of all, it is an obedient companion. Because of its usefulness, the dog has become one of the conspicuous items on the elitist prestige list. Some ruling houses in the Arab world – Jordan and Bahrain for example – are known to have raised very special breeds. Though polluted, the dog in Arab culture is bred for a better and stable blood-line, much like other admired animals such as hawks, camels and horses.

While Islamic jurists agree on the impurity of the dog, they disagree on the circumstances in which it transmits impurity to man. Take, for example, game meat. Some jurists say that game meat can be eaten, even if the dog has consumed part of it; others forbid it if the dog has wounded the prey, or consumed part of its meat, or if the prey has been killed by the dogs' sheer weight.[16] This is in accordance with *sura* 5:4 which states:

> Forbidden to you are: dead meat, blood, pig meat; the meat sacrificed to deities other than God; the meat [of prey] which has been killed by strangling, or by a violent blow, or by a headlong fall, or by being gored to death;[17] the meat partly eaten by wild animals, or slaughtered for divinatory purposes.

The attention paid to the pig and the dog did not change their classification in the impure, polluted category. Hence, the question as to why these animals are classified as such remains unanswered. Following Mary Douglas's work on the subject, I maintain that the answer lies in the classification system itself. After reviewing the forbidden foods in Leviticus, Douglas concludes: 'Those species are unclean which are imperfect members of their class, or whose class itself confounds the general scheme of the world.'[18]

The 'general scheme of the world' is built upon the theory of creation which stipulates that God created land, water and sky and placed in each domain different sets of animals, fish and birds respectively. On land he placed the four-legged animals that hop, jump or walk; in water, the scaled fish that swim with fins; in the sky, two-legged birds that fly with feather wings.[19] Any creature that moves in its domain without using the appropriate locomotion assigned to it is unclean

(Leviticus 11:1–30) and, therefore, should be avoided. Consequently, every creature that crawls or flies on land, flies with four legs or without feather wings, like bats for example, or swims without scales or fins opposes the divine nature of creation. Therefore, it is polluted and cannot be eaten.

However, there are certain categories of animals that do not fit into either one of these classification schemes. To use an Islamic terminology, they do not fit into the canine category with claws and paws, or the 'soft' category that chew the cud and have cloven hooves. The pig, for example, is a four-legged animal with cloven hooves, but unlike its kind, it does not chew the cud. Similarly, the rabbit chews the cud, but unlike its kind, it does not have cloven hooves. In brief, the pig and the rabbit are 'imperfect members of their class'.[20]

The impurity of the dog can be explained by the same principle: it is an animal with canines and claws, but unlike its kind, it has been domesticated and lives in association with man. Therefore, it lies outside the category it belongs to; hence its impurity.

I have gone over these arguments to show that the avoidance of certain species and the acceptance of others does not necessarily relate to one being inherently pure and another inherently polluted, or one being medically beneficial and another harmful. It is rather a matter of classification: either it is incongruous with the theory of divine creation or difficult to classify.

Besides, the division of creatures and things into pure and polluted, like good and bad, high and low, rich and poor, believer or non-believer, is perhaps another manifestation of the dual conception of reality, 'binary opposition', a mentalistic image of the world.[21] The emergence of creatures that cannot be fitted into the divine theory of creation or the dual classification of animals and birds is typically an evolutionary phenomenon, an aspect of the random character of biological evolution. One of the main principles of evolution is that species of plants and animals branch off, change and multiply according to their genetic endowments and the environment in which they live. In brief, there is no master plan for any species to develop in a predictable preconceived line. Evolution is a dynamic process of change through which new species emerge and old species perish. Correspondingly, many physical traits overlap at random from one species to another. For example, modern surgery has shown that the pig, which is considered the most polluted, defiled and unclean creature, seems to have many organs – hearts, kidneys, heart valves, pancreatic cells, veins and arteries – that can be transplanted in man.[22]

The conclusion that impurity, defilement, uncleanness, or pollution is a quality of those who lie outside the mother group to which they should belong, 'the imperfect members of their class', is well documented in the Qur'an. The word *najis* (polluted), as mentioned earlier, occurs only once in *sura* 9:28:

> O ye who believe, truly the polytheists (*mushrikun*) are *najis*, they should not enter The Sacred Mosque.

It is not easy to find a word in English that would convey the meaning of *mushrikun*, *al-shirk* in Islam is the antithesis of the absolute 'oneness' of God who alone must remain the focus of all prayers and rituals.

> Say: He is God, the one and only. God, the Eternal, Absolute. He begeteth not nor is He begotten. And there is none like unto Him.[23]

This monolithic transcendental image of God has led Muslim extremists to abhor the use of music or chant in worship on the grounds that it is a form of *shirk*. As a rule of thumb, all non-Muslims, e.g., Christians, Jews, pagans, or Hindus – could be said to be *mushrikun*. They are polluted because they lie outside the group of the believers, imperfect members of their class.

Besides, Islam is not only a religion that calls for man's salvation; it is a form of brotherhood as well. The Qur'an states categorically:

> The believers are truly a single brotherhood, so establish reconciliation between your brothers.[24]

In my work on Islam in West Africa, one theme repeatedly emerged: a Muslim never fears hunger; he can always lean on his brothers. The concept of regimentation (*al-saff*) is very strong in Islam:

> Truly God loves those who fight for His cause as a single line [regiment] as if they were a single cemented structure.[25]

In his interpretation of this Qur'anic verse, Ibn Kathir says:

> The owner of a building would not like to see contrasts in the structure. So is God, the Glorious, who loves not to see confusion in his message. Truly God has lined up the believers in prayer and in Holy Wars.[26]

To the Arab Muslim mind, the arrangement of people in

lines is an expression of unity and solidarity. It is interesting to note in this regard that unity is often metaphorically described as 'the comb's teeth', 'string of beads', 'chain', or 'cable' as in *sura* 3:103.

And hold fast, all of you together, to the cable [*habl*] of God and do not separate.

Impurity is not only extended to human beings, animals, birds or fish that lie outside their class, but it is also thought to be the quality of behaviour or actions that do not conform to the norm, the familiar practice. Among these practices are: intercourse with a woman during her menstruation period; penetrating her from the anus; having sex or marrying within the forbidden group; intercourse with a beast or a corpse; or eating the meat of an animal with which man had intercourse.[27] All these practices cause defilement, and therefore should be purified by the appropriate standard rituals.

CHAPTER 5

The Impurity of Blood

Impurity is not a static, solid substance; like radiation or contagious diseases, it moves from one dwelling to another through touch and contact, or eating and drinking. The impure remains so until it is purified. All impure animals, birds and fish generate impurity; all the liquids the human body secretes – blood, urine, semen, solid wastes, infected blood, vomit are impure and cause impurity. The human body is shameful and therefore a source of impurities.

According to Islamic law, the believers should purify themselves before prayer, rotating around the Ka'ba in Mecca, and before performing the *'umra* ritual (visiting Mecca outside the prescribed dates for pilgrimage). Because Muslims pray five times a day and every time they pray they have to purify themselves, lengthy treatises are written on the legitimacy of purification rituals. Muslim jurists of different schools of law address this problem meticulously in considerable detail, which subsequently reflects on the centrality of the concepts of purity and pollution in the practice of religion. Perhaps, this concern would not have taken place were it not for the original belief that pollution is an inherent quality in creatures and things.

Of all these impurities, I shall deal here with blood and

semen, if for nothing other than the popular concern with them; people associate blood with life, and semen with procreation. In doing so, I hope to be setting a style of analysis that can be applied to other impurities as well.

Concerning blood, the contradictory, oppositional meanings it signifies are baffling. On the one hand, it stands for nobility, origin, honour, unity of purpose, affinity, love and sometimes for the entire personality, and on the other, it is defiling, polluting and contaminating. While the exchange of blood between two people creates everlasting brotherhood, touching menstrual blood generates impurity. In his work on symbols in African ritual, Turner describes this polarity as a form of 'binary opposition'.[1]

In *sura* 5:4, the impurity of blood is considered equivalent to the impurity of dead meat or pork· 'Forbidden are dead meat, blood, pork . . . etc. that is impiety.' Likewise, *sura* 7:133 dictates:

So We sent on them [the pharaohs] floods, locusts, lice, frogs, and blood as detailed, self-evident signs [or God's wrath]. But they were immersed in arrogance, and were criminals.

In this context, the phrase 'sent on' implies punishment, and blood an instrument of punishment. In other words, God punishes the non-believers by sending them floods, frogs, lice, locusts, blood, [drought] and crop failures.

We punished the Pharaohs with years of crop failures [caused by drought].[2]

Menstrual blood is impure. Consequently menstruating

women are forbidden from having sexual intercourse, holding prayer, or walking round the Holy Ka'ba. They are also forbidden from entering the mosque, resting or sitting in it, or climbing to it. They are not permitted to touch the Qur'an or read the hymns praising the Prophet.[3] 'Only the pure may touch the Qur'an.'[4]

In Islamic *shari'a*, what is said about menstrual blood applies simultaneously to parturition blood – the blood that accompanies the birth of a child.[5]

Likewise, in some eastern churches, menstruating women are forbidden from entering the altar area or partaking of communion because of their impurity. Of course, there is no reference to this practice in the New Testament which, if anything, wipes out impurity altogether from living creatures. The practice seems to be either the making of the early church fathers who were mostly recruited from the class of monks many of whom were celibates with little experience of women, or to have continued from Judaic traditions. According to the Old Testament, menstruating women, like women who give birth to a child, 'shall touch nothing which is holy, and shall not enter the sanctuary till her days of purification are completed'.[6]

> Anyone who touches an impure woman shall be unclean. Everything on which she lies or sits during her impurity shall be unclean.[7]

However, the Antiochian Orthodox Church has recently decided to undo what the early fathers of the church had decreed and abolish the restrictive conditions imposed upon menstruation or parturition.[8]

Just as it stands for impurity, blood may signify noble

origin, social notability, good upbringing, and high honour. In Lebanon, we say 'blood cannot be transformed to water' in praise of somebody's supremacy and outstanding achievements. It is said of people who give generously to charity and good causes, who acquire admirable skills and are willing to pass them to others, or who are prepared to stand by their commitments or champion the cause of the weak and the underprivileged. We also say, 'of the same blood' meaning political unity, solidarity or same origin. In this context, blood becomes synonymous to Ibn Khaldun's 'asabiyah signifying social solidarity. 'Origin' is thought to pass through blood, and genealogies are traced through what is known as 'blood relations'. Thoroughbred horses are referred to as pure-blood horses.

Because genealogies and descent are traced through blood, it can be substituted for genetic relations as in 'blood brotherhood'. Two people, who are not related genetically, could become brothers if they ritualistically exchange blood. They puncture the index finger until it bleeds, then mix their blood together while taking an oath of allegiance. Through the ritualistic exchange of blood, strangers become siblings.

In the same vein, a virgin's blood, unlike menstrual blood, signifies good and honourable upbringing. In a public lecture delivered in the Middle Eastern Hospital in Beirut, Shaikh Muhammad Husain Fadlallah, an eminent Shi'a scholar, asserts: 'According to Islamic law, it is quite legitimate in some specific cases of rape to patch the virginity membrane, for not doing so may expose the girl and her family to unrepairable damage. Everybody, including pilgrims,' he adds, 'have memorized the following verse of poetry: "High honour could not be saved from injury until blood is shed on its sides."'[9]

More likely the pronoun 'its' in this context refers to women's sexual organs, and blood to the blood of virginity. A woman's virginity signifies her and her immediate family's honour; its absence shames her and the family. This is why in some Arab countries, such as Egypt and Yemen, the families of the newly wed couple gather together to celebrate the bride's virginity, which takes place at what is called the 'night of penetration' which marks the official consummation of marriage. The night of penetration in Arab-Islamic tradition is equivalent to the wedding ceremony among Christians. The display of sheets stained with the blood of virginity is a clear attestation to the girl's virginity. The attendants often respond to the display of blood with cries of joy.

Because it sustains honour, virginity raises the dower, and divorce or widowhood, by contrast, lowers it. Upon their second marriage, women are always pledged much lower dower compared to their first marriage when they were virgins.

Like the blood of virginity, the martyr's blood is holy and pure; it is sacrificial blood. Any blood shed for a collective purpose – revenge, vengeance, rebelliousness against tyranny is considered pure. When a Palestinian rebel-terrorist assassinated the late Wasfi al-Tell, the Prime Minister of Jordan, at the entrance of the Hilton Hotel in Cairo following the bloody massacre of the Palestinian fighters in Amman in September 1971, the assassin drank al-Tell's blood, in search of purification. Many a Muslim Arab threatens to feast on the blood of the enemy in an effort to assert his power and authority. The victors always take pride in devouring or shedding the enemy's blood. Ibn Manzur says that the spears that acquire a darker shade in war are called *al-mudama* (the bloody) in reference to the blood staining them – a term derived from *al-damiya* meaning the blessed one.[10] To shed the enemy's blood is a blessing and to shed one's own is the epitome of sacrifice. No wonder that the highest form of love is symbolized by the wounded heart.

In brief, blood symbols seem to cluster in two opposed categories: the pure and the polluted. The pure symbols are associated with voluntary acts: establishing brotherhood pacts, tracing genealogies and origins, displaying virginity tests, making sacrifices in acts of martyrdom, conquest, vengeance, revenge, rebelliousness or love. By contrast, the polluted symbols refer to those instances where blood flows naturally as an inherent quality of creatures, as in menstruation, parturition, running blood, blood poured forth, and in divine forms of punishment in which case it is equivalent to sending lice, drought and frogs.

However, it remains to be stressed that blood impurity forms an integral part of the scheme of classifying creatures and things into pure and polluted, where impurity is thought to be an inherent quality of creatures and things. In Christianity, for example, where the whole concept of impurity is eliminated, the two opposed categories of blood are subsequently forgotten. There exists instead one ritualistic meaning that alludes to sacrifice and repentance. In his letter to the Philippians, Paul writes:

If my life-blood is to crown that sacrifice which is the offering up of your faith, I am glad of it, and I share my gladness with you all.[11]

It is likewise mentioned in John:[12]

> One of the soldiers stabbed His [Jesus's] side with a lance and at once there was a flow of blood and water.

Here, water stands for baptism and blood for the holy sacrifice for the salvation of man. Christians believe that God ordained crucifixion and the shedding of Christ's blood in order to wipe out the sins of man. It is written in Matthew:[13]

> This is my blood, the blood of the covenant shed for many for the forgiveness of sins.

It must be noted at this stage that the offering of sacrificial blood is an old Semitic ritual culminating in Abraham's readiness to offer Isaac, his only son, on the altar for what he thought was God's will:

> There Abraham built an altar and arranged the wood. He bound his son Isaac and laid him on the altar on the top of the wood. Then he stretched out his hand and took the knife to kill his son; but the angel of the Lord called to him from heaven, Abraham, Abraham . . . Do not raise your hand against the boy. Abraham looked up and there he saw a ram caught by its horns in the thicket. He took the ram and offered it as a sacrifice instead of his son.[14]

Sacrificial blood is offered by a person to recompense sins committed by himself or by others. And because blood is strongly linked to life, its offering marks the height of sacrifice. The popular chant, 'We redeem thee by our souls, by our blood,' which is often said in support of political leaders, conveys unconditional political loyalty. In body language, the same meaning is conveyed by a partisan drawing the sign of 'slaughter' around his neck.

In Arab culture, the neck signifies the place where honour, devotion and loyalty are located. To tap a person on the back of his neck is to insult him; the strong threaten to twist or step on the necks of the weak. In Bahrain, the poll tax collected mainly from the Shi'a population before the institution of reforms in the mid-thirties was called *rqabiyah* from *raqba* (neck), thus emphasizing the coercive nature of the tax, and the weak position of the Shi'a.

Likewise, the money paid in compensation for murder is called *diyya* or *fidiya* meaning 'sacrifice' rather than 'blood money', which is the phrase used in the western media. The Arabic word *fidiya* symbolizes the sacrificial nature of the compensation, for blood cannot be compensated by money; it can be 'sacrificed' by money, so to speak. And to reinforce its sacrificial nature, the 'sacrifice money' is often accompanied by a ritualistic meal where the victim's family hosts the murderer's. In other words, 'sacrifice money' is paid for the compensation of sins.

It is written in Genesis:

He who sheds the blood of a man, for that man his blood will be shed [by God], for in the image of God has God made man.[15]

Blood is the property of God, especially the blood of man who is created in God's image. And he who is thus created, God will avenge his murder, which suggests that the 'sacrifice money' paid is ultimately an approach to appeal for God's forgiveness.

Here lies the meaning of crucifixion in Christianity as a

sacrifice to wipe out man's original sin. Through crucifixion, the Lord offers himself as the sacrificial ram to redeem
man's sins. The holy liturgy, which is repeatedly observed in
various churches on Sundays where the blood and flesh of
Christ are symbolically consumed through communion is in
essence no more than a ritual of forgiveness. Why would the
Lord sacrifice himself for man's sins? The only way to appreciate this question is to believe, as Christians do, that God
is love.

CHAPTER 6

The Impurity of Semen

Islamic jurists often use the term *janaba*, which literally means to come beside, or the phrase 'touching women' to mean orgasm, specifically the emission of semen through sexual intercourse, wet dreams or masturbation. Like blood, the symbolism of semen is polarized. On the one hand, it is an instrument of procreation, fertility and continuity of the human race as shown in *sura* 16:72:

> And God has made for you spouses of your own nature, and made of them sons and daughters and grandchildren.

On the other hand, it is a source of defilement that should be purified before prayer, the ritualistic rotation around al-Ka'ba, and before the performance of the *'umra* during pilgrimage.

> If you had orgasm, then purify yourselves . . .[1]

The emission of semen pollutes, but its outcome and prerequisites – sons, children, and the desire of women – constitute the pleasures of this world's life. In the sense of being an instance of pleasure of this world's life, *janaba* becomes equivalent to wealth, perfume, love of leisure and ornamentation. The following Qur'anic verses clearly illustrate the point:

Wealth and sons are the beauty of this world's life.[2]

Know ye that this world's life is but play and amusement, ornamentation and self-pride, and multiplication in wealth and children . . .[3]

It was adorned for people the love of the desire of women . . .[4]

In the last *sura*, the Almighty addresses the 'people' rather than the believers, which suggests that God in this verse is talking to mankind as a whole. Children and sons are often mentioned in the Qur'an in association with wealth, riches, or cattle; the former, wealth, always takes precedence over the latter, children.[5] In other words, wealth before children is the pleasure of this world's life. No wonder that the Qur'an cautions the believers not to let their concern with wealth and children overshadow religious duties and the remembrance of God.

O ye who believe! Do not let your wealth and children divert you from the remembrance of God.[6]

You were so concerned with accumulation [of wealth and children] until ye visited the graves.[7]

Like the Qur'an, Islamic religious culture entices the believers to marry and multiply. In his book of letters al-Jahiz cites many *hadiths* (the word *hadith* always refers to the Prophet's saying) to this effect. Following is a small sample:

Marry and multiply; I shall make you the most numerous among the world's nations.

If you had accomplished your raids successfully, then [proceed] for marriage, marriage and then marriage.

Poor, poor is a man without a wife. Poor, poor is a woman without a husband.

Marry and seek children; they are the fruits of hearts.

Avoid marrying old barren women.[8]

According to al-Jahiz, 'The Prophet was more of a womanizer than any of his contemporaries; and so were other prophets (peace be on their souls) before him.' It is likewise related to 'Umar, the second caliph who was one of the early companions of the Prophet, to have said, 'I shall struggle in marriage until God exacts a breath from me that would praise him.' It is also reported of him to have stated, 'Marry young virgins; they have perfumed mouths, and narrow vaginas.'[9]

Other writers have reported similar *hadiths* focusing on the same theme, the encouragement of marriage.

O ye young men! Whoever amongst you could provide for the dower let him get married; for that would improve his sight and protect his body.[10]

I [The Prophet] pray and sleep; I fast and break fast; I

marry women. Who ever diverts from my traditions does not belong to me.[11]

These sayings do not only encourage people to get married, but also insist on the marriage of virgins. Jabir Bin Abdallah, one of the Prophet's contemporaries, reported:

I married a divorcee. The Prophet asked me, 'Did you get married, Jabir?'
'Yes,' I replied.
'To a virgin or non-virgin?' he inquired.
'Truly, to a non-virgin,' I answered.
He then commented, 'Why not [marry] a youthful virgin who would play with you and you play with her; you would make her laugh and she would make you laugh.'[12]

In another anecdote the Prophet said:

You will be rewarded [in the afterlife] for your intercourse with your wife. They asked, 'We satisfy desire, shall we still be rewarded?'
He answered, 'Yes, for if you had mated with her unlawfully, you would have committed a sin; but if you had mated with her lawfully, you shall be rewarded.'[13]

The Prophet is also reported saying:

Every praise [of God] is an act of alms-giving; every chant of 'God Is Greater' is an act of alms-giving; every prayer is an act of alms-giving; every call for the avoidance of the forbidden is an act of alms-giving; every intercourse [with a wife] is an act of alms-giving.[14]

The last passage not only shows that intercourse is an act of alms-giving, but that in this sense it is equivalent to praising God, chanting the call for prayer, and the command of righteousness and the avoidance of the forbidden.

In the same vein, the Prophet strongly urges the Islamic community to be selective in the choice of spouses. In one of his numerous *hadiths* on the subject, he instructs his followers: 'Be selective of your sperm, for heredity can be deceptive.'[15] According to the Qur'an, the child passes through four stages of growth in the prenatal period:

> We created you out of dust, then out of 'sperm', then 'clot of blood', and then a 'piece of flesh', and finally a 'creature'.[16]

The first stage, which literally means a drop, refers to the sperm, the semen; the second takes place when the sperm changes to a clot of blood; the third when the clot grows into a piece of flesh; the fourth, when the child takes on a visible human form.[17]

Just as the Qur'an considers children to be 'the beauty of this world's life', it correspondingly made it possible for men to mate with their wives whenever they desired.

> Your wives are your tilth, so approach your tilth when and how you so wish, but do good beforehand, and fear God . . .[18]

The phrase 'when and how you wish' suggests that intercourse for pleasure is permissible. In his book *The Interpretation of the Qur'an*, al-Sayyuti explains this verse in the following words:

Tilth is the place of planting the child. 'Approach your tilth when and how you so wish' [is a statement that] refers to the position a person may take during intercourse: standing, sitting or lying; and either from the front or the back. 'And do good beforehand' means you have to mention the name of God before intercourse.[19]

To mention the name of God is to say: 'By the name of God the merciful and compassionate' before commencing on an action be it intercourse, eating, drinking, walking, opening a conference or making a speech.

The phrase 'to approach women from the back' does not mean to have anal intercourse with women, which is strictly forbidden in Islam, it is to have intercourse while the woman is in a special position (*mujbat*) – 'lying down on her belly with her hands on the floor, her face downward, and half-standing on her knees'.[20] All schools in Islam consider mating in the anus an unlawful, evil act.[21] As a matter of fact, the Qur'an clearly speaks against it:

> Keep away from women during menstruation, and do not approach them until they are purified. But when they have purified themselves, then approach them [have intercourse] in the place where God has ordered you.[22]

The consensus among jurists is that the phrase 'where God has ordered you' refers to the vagina.[23]

It is on this basis that Islamic law disapproves of homosexuality, lesbian relationships or 'rubbing' which refers to reaching orgasm by rubbing the male organ against the female's. In Islamic *shari'a* these acts are treated as crimes and subsequently receive the same penalties as adultery. Thus, an offender who commits any of these crimes, when witnessed by four persons, may receive the death penalty, or be stoned or whipped depending upon the circumstances prevailing at the time. Should the crime be committed against a person whom the offender is forbidden to marry – daughter, sister, daughter or son's daughter, sister or brother's daughter – the offender would receive the death penalty and he would be killed by the sword; this is irrespective of whether or not he is a 'fortressed' man. Legally, a 'fortressed' person is a free man, not a slave, who is married to a woman whom he has penetrated and is capable of having intercourse with her whenever and however he wishes. A 'fortressed' woman, on the other hand, is married and has a husband who has penetrated her, and who is living with her.

On the other hand, should the offender be 'unfortressed' and have committed the crime against a person who does not belong to the forbidden group, he will be whipped one hundred lashes. A virgin girl, who by definition is 'unfortressed', would likewise be whipped one hundred lashes under the same circumstances.[24]

Intercourse with menstruating women is forbidden. Ibn Kathir reports that when the Prophet was asked about approaching menstruating women, he responded, 'Do whatever you wish minus intercourse.' Ibn Kathir then tells the following anecdote about 'A'isha, the Prophet's most favoured wife, who said:

When the Prophet felt he was cold, and happened to be in my house, he asked me to come closer to him. I said: 'I am in my menstruation period.' He then said, 'Uncover your leg.' I did. And then he put his head and shoulder in my lap until he warmed up and thereafter he slept.[25]

Islam discusses sexual matters openly and without re-
serve. Sex or having sex are treated as natural givens, 'Innate
ingredients of the human psyche, intrinsic desires joined to
man upon his creation'.[26] Because the body is treated as a
source of shame or impurities it is continuously inspected,
checked and examined for purification purposes.

However, the tendency to deal with sex as a natural given
is often obscured by notions about women and sex in general. Women are thought to be replete with mystery and
secrecy. In his work on *The Insurance of Sex in Islam*,
Sulaiman al-Yahfufi writes:

A woman is a secret flowing in the veins of men continuously transmitting vague senses from an unknown world.[27]

He adds:

Sexual desire is an insisting instinct that bites.[28]

It constitutes one of two types of hunger: sex and belly.
[There exist] two vacuums that preoccupy the minds of
the Islamic community: sex and food.[29]

Women are 'secrets', 'hungers', 'riddles' and 'vacuums'.
Al-Jahiz, the famous man of letters of the ninth century,
quotes Sahib al-Ghilman as saying:

If man befriends a woman she will grey his hair, destroy
his scent, blacken his skin, and increase his urine. Women
are the traps of the devil and the [tricky] ropes of Satan.[30]

To liken sex to Satan is not an unfamiliar equation in Arab-Islamic sources. In one of his *hadiths*, the Prophet advises:

> Beware of seeking solitude with women, I swear by He who holds my soul in his hands, that soon as a man seeks solitude with a woman, Satan instantly enters between them.[31]

More likely, Satan in this context stands for sexual desire.

Clearly, Islam openly urges believers to marry, have intercourse and multiply. To have intercourse with one's wife is equivalent to alms-giving, and will be rewarded in the afterlife. The desire for women is one of this world's pleasures, and it is not entirely absent in the afterlife. The Qur'an promises the believers a place in paradise where 'they shall have joy in all they do; they and their spouses resting in the shade on reclining thrones'.[32]

For the pious men, God has also created a class of very special women: virgins, who are equal [to their husbands] in age, and who sexually desire their husbands out of love and devotion.[33] This special breed of women, who are promised for the pious in heaven, are described in the Qur'an as having 'big, wide eyes like pearls'[34] – qualities that signify the height of beauty in Arab culture.

The literature in Islam that encourages believers to marry, mate, desire women and beget children is coupled by a collection of traditions calling for the control of the sex drive, and the building of equitable relationships between spouses. It is stated in the Qur'an:

> And of His works, He created for you mates from among

yourselves, so that you may dwell in tranquillity with them. And He has established loyalty and mercy between you.[35]

In another text, God says in the Qur'an: 'They [wives] are your garments, and you [husbands] are their garments'.[36] Therefore, just as a wife is a dwelling of tranquillity and a moral cover for her husband, so is he for her. In this context, 'garment' refers to the public image. In other words, husbands and wives should take into account each other's psychological and sexual needs. Rashid Rida, the Islamic reformist of the nineteenth century, put it:

> The psychological and sexual satisfaction between husband and wife is an expression of their mutual loyalty and affection. Its attainment enhances their humanity, and moderates deeply felt mental disturbances.[37]

Indeed, sexual satisfaction occupies a very special place in Islam. In a sense, it is equivalent to eating and drinking as shown in the directives for fasting during Ramadan:

> And seek what God has ordained for you. And eat and drink until the white thread of dawn appears distinct from the black thread. Then complete your fast till the night [of the second day] appears, but do not approach your wives while you are in retreat.[38]

In other words, sexual intercourse during the fasting month of Ramadan is governed by the same rules for eating and drinking. In general, sexual life is so central to the practice of religion in Islam that a large body of the *hadiths* address the issue in meticulous detail. The theme, repeated several times, is how to maintain an active sexual relationship between husband and wife. I shall briefly discuss some of these *hadiths* if for nothing other than their historical value, which reflects some of the main ideas then current about sexual life.

The Prophet is reported to have said, 'There are five elements to sex appeal: circumcision [of males and females], shaving the pubic hair, plucking armpit hair, cutting and polishing fingernails, and pruning the moustaches.'[39] Female circumcision is believed to enhance sexual pleasure provided that a small part of the clitoris is cut.[40] In an anecdote related to Umm Attiya:

> The Prophet told a woman who was circumcising females in al-Madina, 'Shorten your cuts and do not exaggerate, for that is better for the female and highly appreciated by the male'.[41]

Scientifically speaking, there is no evidence to believe that female circumcision (clitoridectomy) enhances sexual pleasure. On the contrary, the evidence shows that it complicates childbirth causing higher rates of female mortality.

In another anecdote related to 'A'isha, the Prophet said:

> There are ten elements to sexual charm: pruning the moustache, trimming the beard, cleaning the teeth, cutting and polishing the nails, washing the mouth, washing the finger joints, plucking the armpit hair, shaving the pubic hair, and gargling with water.[42]

In the same vein, he advises the Muslim community:

Wash your clothes, have regular haircuts, clean your teeth, decorate your bodies, and wash regularly. The Israelites fail to do so; in consequence their women adulterated.[43]

In another story, the Prophet told a man whose hair and beard were left unattended 'to mend them for that would be better than looking like Satan'.[44] Of special importance are the *hadiths* that encourage women to decorate themselves for their husbands. In one of these *hadiths* reported by Ibn Kathir, the Prophet said:

I don't like to look at a woman with no tattoos on her hand and no kohl on her eyes.[45]

However, he spoke of moderation in the use of ornaments, in the sense that it would not change the looks of what God has created and what nature has delivered. Hence, the *hadith*:

May God's curse fall upon the women who change their pigmentation, who pluck their faces, and who grate their front teeth.

The first reference is to women who try to change the colour of their skin by the use of needles or artificial drugs; the second to those who pluck the hair of their faces especially the eyebrows; the third to those who grate their teeth in an effort to look younger than their age.[46] The use of cosmetics is tolerated as long as it aims to enhance a woman's femininity and soften her roughness. Under no condition should women behave like men. The Prophet insisted that the following will never be taken care of on the day of resurrection: 'the person who fails to serve his parents, the pimp who lures customers to his prostitute wife, and the women who mimic men.'[47] Women are requested not to imitate men in the way they dress, walk, talk or in other body movements.

In his book on *Marriage Life According to the Islamic Shari'a*, al-Sawwaf affirms that sexual arousal can be attained through sight, touch, smell, and thought, and that sight is more effective among men than women who are generally seduced by touch. Because they are deeply moved by sight, there are few men who could control themselves when they see a naked woman. He adds: 'Most rape cases take place when a man is confronted with the beauty of a woman's naked or semi-naked body'.[48] Therefore, it is imperative that women do not display the beauty of their bodies to anyone other than their husbands. This is precisely what is meant by the term *'urub*, the modest women who, out of love and devotion, surrender and expose their bodies only to their husbands.

However, Islamic jurists are not in agreement as to whether or not a man should look at his wife's naked body. Some permit it, some oppose it, and some admit that although not forbidden, it is detestable. When Uthman bin Madh'un told the Prophet about his bashfulness looking at his wife's naked body, the Prophet commented, 'Why not, God has made you her garment and made her your garment.'[49] This view is supported by 'A'isha who is reported to have said, 'The Prophet and I used to bathe together in the same tub while making love.'[50] Contrarily, she is also reported saying, 'I have never yet seen the Prophet's naked body.'[51]

Although I have not taken a statistical count of the *hadiths* it seems that a larger number of jurists did not approve of a man looking at his wife's naked body. Some advised, 'When you mate with your wife do not look at her genitalia; this will cause blindness'.[52] Others added, 'Looking at the wife's naked body causes blindness, and talking to her [during intercourse] causes muteness'.[53] In other words, don't look and don't talk while making love to your wife. Ibn Maja cites a *hadith* saying, 'When any one of you approaches his wife, he shall not do so nakedly as two camels'.[54]

In brief, while the Malikiyah school of law allowed the spouses to look at each other's naked bodies, the Shafi'iyah considered it detestable behaviour, and the Hanbaliyah forbade it altogether. The consensus among jurists is to be modest during intercourse. The question of who amongst the believers obeys the dictates of the school of law to which he belongs remains unanswered. I am sure it varies with personal religiosity, whims, mood and social background.

Concerning smell, the Prophet repeatedly encouraged Muslims to use perfume. Of his famous *hadiths* on the subject: 'Two things in this world earned my love and affection, women and perfume.'[55] In this sense, he made perfume symbolically equivalent to women. In an anecdote about a woman who asked him about purification from menstrual blood, he responded, 'Take a piece of musk and purify yourself with it'.[56] Of course, this *hadith* goes contrary to the official Islamic law that requires for purification purposes, especially in the cases of menstruation, parturition or the flow of semen, the use of absolute water, and in the absence of water the use of earth or sand. He was perhaps because of his fondness for fragrance that the Prophet insisted on shaving the pubic hair and plucking the armpit hair, the sources of bad smell.

Touch is another aspect of sexual life which Islamic jurists have discussed in some detail. It not only refers to sexually sensitive areas such as the neck, the ear, the nipple, the clitoris and the like, but it also includes simple and some-times innocent gestures, for example shaking hands, touching shoulders, or any other form of body contact between the sexes. In Islam it is forbidden for a woman to shake hands with a man other than her immediate family, especially if she has fulfilled the duty of pilgrimage. Customarily, how-ever, many a woman covers her hand with a scarf while shaking hands with a friend who is not a family member.

Any physical contact between men and women, accord-ing to al-Sawwaf, is likely 'to add fuel to fire; it is the fastest way of sexual arousal'.[57] Of course, this directive does not apply to husband and wife who are encouraged to 'play' be-fore sexual intercourse, as mentioned earlier.

In the face of all these discussions about sexual life, the question remains: what is it that constitutes impurity in love making?

Some jurists, like Imam al-Rida for example, believe that impurity takes place when the two circumcised organs touch.[58] Males are circumcised by cutting the skin that cov-ers the head of the penis, and females by cutting the clitoris or part of it. However, most jurists agree that impurity oc-curs when the head of the penis penetrates the vulva irrespective of whether or not orgasm is reached, or when the semen flows either in or outside the vagina. And it makes no difference whether the semen flows slowly or in abun-dance, with or without lust, or during sleep.

In brief, impurity takes place through the flow of semen during intercourse, masturbation or wet dreams. In an un-verified *hadith*, it is said, 'The fucker of his hand [masturbator] will not be seen on the day of resurrection'.[59] However, many jurists ruled that it is legally permissible for men to be masturbated by their wives, but mentioned noth-ing about the masturbation of women by their husbands.

The rules and directives that govern impurity among men apply to women in precisely equal terms. Some writers, like Knaifani for example, are of the opinion that women can easily reach orgasm and that they require a 'simple friction of legs for a short period of time to experience orgasm'.[60] He adds, a woman may reach orgasm even if she 'rides a bicycle or exposes herself to the vibrations of a train'.[61]

It must be stressed however, that these fancy, exaggerated expectations of women's sexual behaviour reflect Arab cultural dictum rather than a physiological reality. In fact, women are known for their relative slowness in reaching orgasm: while male orgasm takes place in a single discharge, women experience it gradually in successive stages.

What I have discussed so far constitutes only a small part of the extensive literature on sexual life in Islam. The Qur'anic verses, the *hadiths*, the stories and the anecdotes I have cited are meant to present a sample of the kind of work done on the subject.

It is clearly noticeable that while the literature on sexual life encourages marriage, play and laughter before intercourse, the desire for women, and to regard love-making equivalent to alms-giving that deserves a divine reward in the afterlife, it simultaneously condemns the results of orgasm, the flow of semen.

Like running blood, in the case of menstruation and other instances, the flow of semen is a pollutant that must be purified before prayer and the performance of other Islamic rituals. According to Islamic *shari'a*, the rules that govern menstruation and parturition govern likewise the attainment of orgasm and the flow of semen. In other words, the polluted person is not allowed to pray, fast, walk around al-Ka'ba, touch or read the Qur'an or the poetry recited in praise of God and his Prophet. He is also forbidden from entering or staying in the mosque.[62] It is related that Imam al-Sadiq said:

> Purification by washing the body after orgasm is an absolute requirement; the person who intentionally leaves a single hair unwashed will be doomed to fire.[63]

However, unlike blood which pollutes only when it flows involuntarily, semen pollutes irrespective of whether it flows in intercourse and masturbation, or involuntarily as in wet dreams. It is perhaps because of its polluting character that many a believer asks for God's forgiveness before approaching his wife as if he is committing an evil act. Yet, Muslims know that intercourse is a source of life, and to reconcile the dilemma they perform a short prayer, kneeling twice, before making love. In this prayer, they appeal to God in the following words:

> O God! I ask thee to bestow upon me her [my wife] intimacy, loyalty and affection. Helping us to stand together united in cooperation, for you love the lawful and hate the forbidden.[64]

Then the husband puts his hand over his wife's head and adds while facing Mecca:

> O God! In your trust I took her, and in your words I married her. O God! Make her a loyal, child-bearing woman who knows no hatred, eats from what is available, and inquires not about what has already passed.[65]

Like blood that flows for a noble cause, prayer and the appeal to God may help nullify the polluting effects of semen, thus rendering it an admissible instrument for the continuity of the human race. After all, children are the joy of this world's life.

PART II

_____

BODY LANGUAGE

CHAPTER 7

The Body as a Medium of Communication

The belief that the body is a source of shame in Islam has, in my opinion, greatly shaped its utility as a medium of communication – body language. The elite class, who present themselves as models of behaviour, rarely resort to gestures or body movement to assert or deny what they say. To talk while moving your hands, body and legs exaggeratedly in different directions creates suspicion; it is befitting only of loose, dubious characters. In their public councils, men of power and status (kings, sultans, emirs or *shuyukh*) give orders or respond to questions and inquiries with minimal gestures or body movement. With their Arabian *thawb* (men's dress) covering the body from top to toe, they look to the foreign eye as if they were statues made of marble with porcelain glazed faces.

In fact, the face and the fingers, the only visible parts of the body, play the major role in communication; the eyes and the index finger are mostly used for this purpose. With a nod, a wink, or a subtle finger movement, an emir instructs his attendants to welcome guests, seat them in the proper places, serve coffee, usher them out, or simply stay silent.

As you enter his council, the emir stares at you in order to humble you, to tell you that he is in charge. It would be impolite for you to stare back, for to do so is to challenge his authority. In his council, the emir is the sole authority. The Qur'anic injunction 'lower your gaze' is meant to establish propriety among commoners rather than telling the emir how to conduct the business of power. Staring signifies a power relationship: the dominant stares and the dominated lowers the gaze, looks downward at the floor or sideways. In traditional communities, women always look downward as a sign of deference and respect to men, and men do so in respect to their superiors. Parenthetically, documentary data among animals in the wild show that the weak give way to the strong by using the same gestures, lowering the gaze.

I shall discuss these gestures and body movements in more details in the coming chapters. The point I want to make here is that it is not a mere coincidence that the face and fingers play the major role in body communication in Arab-Islamic culture. On the contrary, it is an outcome of trying to protect the *farj*. When women put on 'Islamic dress', they leave nothing visible of the body other than the face and the fingers. Although Muslim Arabs use other gestures and body positions to communicate a wide range of meanings, interpreting their meaning is a matter of awareness and frequency of usage. While putting my observations to the test, I discovered that many people were not aware of the range of meanings they convey through body language. They were able to recognize mostly the meanings of facial expressions, but were not very keen on the observation of social distance and the more subtle gestures and body positions that convey attentiveness, boredom, generosity, thrift, and the like. No wonder that *al-farasa* in Arabic, the ability to read body language, is practically confined to reading only facial expressions.

What is Body Language?

Communication is made through three different but related vehicles: language, sign language and body language. Language refers to communication through the manipulation of different sound systems produced by articulations made in the oral cavity, involving the tongue, teeth, lips, lungs, oesophagus, pharynx, nose and the vocal cords. To call language a 'tongue' is using the part to stand for the whole, since the tongue is only one of many organs involved in speech. In fact, phonemes, the meaningful units of sound that combine to form morphemes or words, are produced by making identifiable articulations. The 'p' sound, for example, is produced by pressing the lips together, whereas the 's' sound by pressing the teeth together. Linguists could describe the exact articulations involved in every single letter of the alphabet of every language.[1]

It must be stressed, however, that communicating through sound systems is not confined to man alone; other creatures do the same. In his work on gorillas, George Schaller was able to identify a large number of utterances they use to locate food, announce the coming of danger and the readiness to mate, fight or play. This is in addition to various gestures and body movements they produce to clarify or underscore oral communication.[2]

Apparently all animals and insects that live in societies – elephants, lions, wild dogs, wolves, apes, ants and bees, pass information to fellow members through a specialized system of communication. In his work on bees, for example,

Alexander Deans found that members of a beehive are able to pass information to others about location and distance of nectar by performing a 'tail wagon' dance which follows figure eight. The intensity of the dance indicates the distance, the farther the nectar from the beehive the higher the intensity of the dance per second. The location is conveyed by performing the dance always at a perpendicular angle to the sun. This is why bees work only in daytime. What we thought to be noisy babble in the beehive seems to be a very specialized code of communication.[3] It is called 'tail' dance because the sound the bee emits is produced by a tiny tail-like organ located at its rear.

The fact that societal animals and insects have developed a peculiar system of communication does not mean that theirs is similar to man's. The difference is one of kind, depending upon the position of the species on the evolutionary scale. The human language is characterized by thirteen different traits some of which are shared with mammals, reptiles and insects; some with a wide variety of apes; some with the hominids (the extinct human-like species); and some are peculiar to man, homo sapiens (see the table in the appendix).

Charles Darwin was the first to draw attention to the importance of body language in the study of evolution. Its importance, as observed by his successors, did not emerge only from its linkage to the theory of the evolution of species, but also from being an integral part of the theory of communication.[4] They noted that a large part of information exchanged between people is carried out through gestures and body movements. Rarely, if ever, do people exchange ideas orally without using gestures and body movements to emphasize, deny, cast doubt, conceal or explain the spoken word.

Indeed, many of us use body language to reflect our speech, such as moving our hands or fingers in circles when we talk about the cyclic nature of life from birth to death, or moving the hand up and down when stressing the boom-bust cyclicity of the economy. Wanting a glass of water, we may imitate the act of drinking, wanting food we mimic the act of eating. It is perhaps possible to find a gesture or body movement for every meaning we express orally.

Using gestures as substitutes for the spoken word may at times acquire a widespread distribution. Whether you are in Lebanon, France, Nigeria, or Brazil, look at the waiter in the restaurant after you finish your meal and move your hand and fingers as though writing, he will bring you the bill. Likewise, while talking about corruption, a twist of the wrist towards the pocket coupled by a sly wink suggests illegal earnings. However, these gestures acquire their meaning from the context, outside the situation they become meaningless.

Although interlinked, language and body language each has its own special domain, its own rules and regulations. Whereas language is used to pass information and convey meaning, body language simultaneously expresses how people react positively or negatively to such information and meanings. A person who reads body language well can judge his audience's response, and can subsequently alter his approach as necessary.

Having its own special domain, body language takes on, exactly like language, standard patterns that are transmitted down generations. These patterns vary according to culture, age, sex, status and individual idiosyncrasies within the same culture. Take, for example, the meanings of kissing. In Arab-Islamic culture, a man kissing another on the cheek is socially and morally acceptable; in fact it is encouraged under certain circumstances. It reflects amity and devotion between friends, neighbours or relatives, and indicates equality of status between interactors. In other words, when Yasir Arafat, the President of the Palestinian Council, approaches British Prime Minister Tony Blair for a kiss, he is not declaring love and affection, but claiming equality of status. Real strangers in the Middle East avoid kissing, and the strong do not kiss the weak. They simply shake hands, or pass by the host while placing their hands on their chest and slightly bending their heads forward as a sign of respect.

Unlike kissing the cheek, kissing the hand implies differentiation in power and authority. It is customary for the son to kiss his father's hand; the novice his tutor's; the young his elder's; the faithful his master's; and the client his patron's. Kissing the hand has acquired this meaning simply because 'hand' is a symbol of authority: 'The hand of God is over their hands'.[5] We say, 'He/she rules with an iron hand,' meaning with firmness and determination.

In brief, the meaning of the kiss, like all other gestures, varies with the context. On the cheek, it signifies amity and equality; on the hand, subordination. While the son kisses his father's hand to show respect and deference, the father reciprocates by kissing the son on the forehead to affirm his affection and love.

It happens in some Arab countries, as in the Gulf for example, that the kiss conveys a multitude of meanings depending on who kisses whom and where. Like *khuwwa*, which is the tax the weak pay to the strong for protection, kissing is subject to the same principle of unstructured reciprocity where the exchange between giver and receiver does not take place in kind and degree. In other words, it raises the status of the receiver and lowers the status of the giver. The emir accepts kisses; he does not kiss. He is kissed by people who are loyal to him; he, in turn, accepts their advances with a comforting smile.

People kiss the emir on the forehead to express their respect for his wisdom; on the shoulder to express their readiness to side with him in times of conflict; on the nose in admiration of his pride and self-esteem. The 'shoulder' signifies collaboration and unity, hence the phrase 'shoulder to shoulder' meaning solidarity in crises. The 'nose' is a symbol of self-esteem, the adjective of which (*anuf*) refers to an assertive person. By contrast, the phrase 'they rubbed his nose on the floor' means they insulted or overwhelmed him.

The meaning of the kiss becomes more complex as we move from the world of men to the world of women. In Arab-Islamic culture, men kissing women is a very private matter; it belongs to married life. In religiously traditional communities, even shaking hands, not to mention kissing, across the gender line is suspicious. True, there are men and women today who do not hesitate to exchange kisses on the cheek, or men who kiss the hands of women out of politeness and respect; however, this they do following modern western customs rather than Arab-Islamic traditions.

There remains kissing on the lips, otherwise referred to as 'the French kiss', which carries purely sexual connotations. In his work *Body Talk*, Desmond Morris asserts that the French kiss between men and women is universally practised as an integral part of sexual life.[6] Some lovers practice it in the open as in Europe and America, and some in private between husband and wife.

Body language is culture-bound, and therefore, the same gesture may convey different meanings in different cultures. Whereas men kissing men signifies amity and friendship ties in Arab culture, in many western societies outside the Mediterranean it often indicates a homosexual commitment.

What is said about kissing correspondingly applies to many other gestures and body movements. Take, for example, smiling. In Arab culture, people exchange smiles in recognition of an old friendship or acquaintance, or as a sign of sharing some hidden understanding between two interactors, which is not shared with the other members of the group. They may also smile sarcastically in disagreement with somebody else's ideas.

By contrast, a man smiles at a woman only to express some sort of admiration; if she positively reciprocates, that would be an invitation to pursue the matter further. If she ignores his smile altogether, that would put an end to his advance. In America a woman smiling at a man or reciprocating his smile may mean nothing other than being polite. This is what many an Arab student in the States continuously fails to appreciate. When some students try to pursue the polite smile further, they may be disappointed.

Although body language varies according to culture, there have emerged a number of gestures and body movements that have acquired standard meanings in all cultures. The whole world laughs for joy and cries for grief, frowns for anger and displays the teeth for aggression. What makes people laugh, cry, frown or display their teeth varies, but the physical response is the same. Everywhere people shrug their shoulders to express uncertainty and indifference, or nod the head to show agreement, or lift it or move it sideways to declare rejection. It is believed that some of these gestures, such as shaking the head sideways to express rejection, is an inherited trait since the deaf and the blind voluntarily and spontaneously use the same gestures to convey the same meaning without being able to learn it by imitation or deliberate instruction.

Whatever the case, the number of gestures having a universal distribution is quite limited. Much like language, body language is culture-bound despite the distribution of many words universally through radio, telephone, computer and fax. With the coming of the computer age and the expanding processes of globalization this will ever be on the increase. Also, like words in a sentence, gestures and body movements do not occur in isolation; they come in clusters. Consider the nuances of a wink in illustration.

We wink as we try to escape from danger, in reacting to a flashing light, in agreement with a point made in conversation, in adoring a pretty girl, in remembrance of a secret kept between friends, or in being critical of somebody else's personality. In the first two instances, the wink is simply a physiological reflex that carries no particular meaning. In the other instances, on the other hand, it is meaningful and tends to occur in association with other gestures and body movements. A wink at a beautiful girl, for example, is often associated with a relaxed facial expression, a broad smile, widening the eyelids, and dilating the pupils. Contrarily, a wink indicating secrecy between friends is often performed with a constrained facial expression, and narrowed eyebrows, lids and contracted pupils.

Although body language has standard patterns that vary according to culture, age, sex, and status, these variations are subject to individual choices and preferences. Like speakers of the same language, who each has his own style of speaking, his own intonation, pronunciation, and sentence construction, so is the case with body language. Within the standard framework, there exist individual styles, personality mazeways (ways that are repeatedly done), that can be detected and enacted. As a matter of fact, imitation of idiosyncratic gestures and body movements, otherwise called

'mirroring'[7] reflects people's evaluation of each other. To be
an object of imitation or mimicking is, in many ways, to be
admired. This is true in love relationships as well as in political loyalty and allegiance. For a girl or a boy to mimic
each other's idiosyncratic gestures is an admission of deep
affection. This also applies to a student who involuntarily
apes his tutor, a novice mirroring his *shaikh*, a client mimicking his patron, or an apprentice imitating his master.
Mirroring may take place through a little gesture, a word or
a phrase; or in the way we sit, stand, eat, or drink.

The important thing is to be able to observe and recognize the gesture when it happens. Nobody is born with an
innate capacity to observe body language; it is an acquired
skill.

Generally speaking, it is possible to deal with body language under two headings: (1) body posture and position
where the body as a whole is observed and analysed, and (2)
the wide scope of gestures and body movements. The first
focus on social distance and the strategy of sitting; the second on sexual symbols and a wide range of moods and
temperaments that people exhibit during their daily interactions. I shall deal with body posture first, and then gesture.

CHAPTER 8

Social Distance and the Confrontational Line

While interacting with others, people always try to keep some distance, a line of confrontation, that sets them apart. The distance may be lengthened or shortened, widened or narrowed, depending upon the type of relationships that bind the interactors together: the closer the distance the higher the level of intimacy; the farther the distance, the lower the level. A mother cuddles her baby and holds him tight to her chest; she smells him and kisses him (sometimes on the genitals) as if he is part and parcel of her own personality. She may do so only to her lover; with others she is reserved, cautious, and weighs her choices several times before committing herself to a definite course of action. She fears that if she moves close to others she may be accused of softness, and if she stays afar and aloof she may be charged with being hard. To strike a balance between the two positions is not easy; many matters related to image and self-image, honour and self-appraisal, are taken into account.

What bewilders the mother concerns every individual in society. We interact with others from a cautious standpoint that implicitly or explicitly defines the nature of our relationships, and subsequently the social distance; whether we

should move close or stay afar. We feel threatened and un-
easy if the safety zone, or the confrontational line, we draw
for ourselves is overtaken by other interactors. This feeling
of uneasiness increases if we find ourselves struggling to enter
into or exit from a narrow door, walking in a crowded street,
or caught amidst an unruly mob. The popular Arabic expression, 'narrows the level of endurance', is a clear
indication of the anxiety that might befall a person once his
safety zone is overwhelmed. Indeed, narrowing the distance
narrows the scale of tolerance.

The confrontational line, the line beyond which we feel
threatened, varies according to species, environment and
culture. Documentaries on various animals, birds and insects
– lions, parrots and snakes – living in the wild have shown
that they defensively charge against a perceived enemy only
if the line of confrontation, which is a measurable distance,
is trespassed. Hence, the popular saying, 'If you corner the
cat, it scratches.'

In human societies, the line of confrontation, the safety
zone, varies according to culture: what troubles a European,
for example, may be quite acceptable to an Arab. It is believed that Europeans feel uncomfortable should they be
approached within a distance of less than half a metre.[1]
Within this distance, they feel that their privacy is invaded,
which threatens their personal sovereignty; and to counter-
balance this affront they spontaneously move away to a safer
distance.

Arabs, on the other hand, seem to be more tolerant of
close, congested distances; no wonder that they crowd rather
than queue for services. Their tolerance, however, is limited
by age, sex, and social standing. Social distance is inversely
related to age: the narrower the distance the wider the differentiation in age. The elderly interact very closely with the

young irrespective of whether or not they are blood relatives. Differentiation in age softens the rigidity of complex and formal interactions and generates a sense of amity. No wonder that heads of states visiting foreign lands are often welcomed by a youngster carrying a bouquet of flowers. This gesture is intended, at least temporarily, to suspend formality and create an atmosphere of good will which is hoped to facilitate negotiations between strangers.

Compared to age, gender differentiation works in the opposite direction; it is governed more by rules of segregation than interaction. In Arab-Islamic culture, men and women have their own private domain inside and outside the house: men interacting with men and women with women. Here society does not pair, as it does in western cultures.[2] In keeping with tradition, society in Arab-Islamic culture allows pairs only in bed. Within the same house, men's domain lies in the reception room or outside it in the open courtyard, and women's domain in the kitchen or the bedroom.[3] Because of this segregation, architectural designs of traditional houses often include two entrances, one leading to the reception room and the other to the kitchen. If it happens, as it sometimes does among the modern sector, that men and women meet in the same room, men cluster on one side and women on the other, each conversing with their own sex.

The principle of segregation is extended to include veiling in its various forms, sometimes covering all the body from head to toe, sometimes only the head and the face, sometimes the head with the face exposed and sometimes the face with the eyes exposed. In public, men walk ahead of women at a distance of no less than a metre. I was told that the religious *shaikhs* among the Druzes walk ahead of their wives

Figure 1
A woman adopting a positive attitude towards a man.

at a distance of no less than forty steps.[4] In the same vein, the sexes are often segregated in schools, universities, hospitals, mosques, markets and sometimes in restaurants and places of entertainment. When I was conducting fieldwork in Bahrain in 1974–75, the Islamic block were protesting against male doctors attending to women patients in hospitals.

For a woman or a man to come within a distance of half to one metre of one another is a clear sign of a positive, favourable attitude. A close distance signifies intimacy, and touch suggests hope and desire. The contrary is also true:

Figure 2
A woman adopting a negative attitude towards a man.

seeking farther or wider distance symbolizes lack of interest and rejection. These opposed attitudes are often reinforced by different body positions. In displaying a positive attitude, the woman approaches the man with her entire body facing him; the feet open at a slanted acute angle with the tip of the toe pointing towards the man as if she is ready to 'walk' into him (*figure 1*).

By contrast, if she stands relatively far off while her body is leaning sideways and her feet pointing to the outside, as if she is walking out of his zone, she is then displaying a negative attitude (*figure 2*).

Social standing in society also modifies social distance: the wider the discrepancy in status between interactors the wider the distance; the narrower the discrepancy, the closer the distance. The arrangement of the seating order in an emir's council in the Gulf countries illustrates the point clearly. Celebrities often sit beside the emir who usually occupies the central part of the council facing the entrance. The highest in status take on the seat to the right of the emir; the left hand, being unclean as it is traditionally used for toilet purposes, assumes a secondary value. As you move away from the emir's seat, the social standing of people begins to gradually drop down to the level of guards and servants who occupy positions at the entrance. Bewildered by their newly acquired status, however, the nouveau riche try to seek pre-eminence by insisting that they be seated beside the emir, regardless.

Social distance is not only modified by differentials in age, sex and social standing; it is equally affected by a variety of moods and relationships that prevail within the interacting group. In this connection, it is possible to distinguish between four types of interaction; (1) the intimate, (2) the social or socializing, (3) the formal used mainly in protocol, and (4) the lecture type.[5] It must be stressed at the outset, however, that in as much as these fields of interaction reflect particular moods and relationships they can be manipulated to generate the very moods and relationships they reflect.

We deal with the intimate field of interaction as if it is the locus of our honour and dignity; only those who are linked to us sentimentally such as parents, family, friends and lovers will be admitted to it. Distance in this field of interaction could become so close as to culminate in physical contact. This applies to interaction between people irrespective of age, sex, or even status. The Islamic rules that forbid marriage between close relatives, brother's daughter, sister's daughter, mother's daughter, father's daughter, and others, allows for intimate interaction to take place without sexual advances.

Just as we express our love and affection through decreasing distance, we simultaneously expose our disappointments by increasing distances. In childhood, playmates sever their relationships by locking the small fingers together, and shake hands upon reconciliation. This is interesting; it suggests that we cut relations in parts, as symbolized by the small finger, and reconcile our conflict in their totality, as symbolized by the whole hand.

The social or socializing field of interaction is often practised in private parties where people seek to cement old relationships or make new ones. Here the distance narrows by virtue of the occasion itself, which allows for relaxed social intercourse to take place and a suspension of formality. The pressure to be 'nice' and cooperative is so strong in this sphere of interaction that many promises made in the evening are broken or forgotten the next day in the morning.

One of the most common forms of the socializing type of interaction takes place in sharing meals. There is some magic in sharing food, eating together, partaking of the same meal. The sacrificial meal among the ancient Semites, communion in the Holy Liturgy among Christians where the body of Christ is symbolically consumed, the *adha* feast in Islam where the rich share food with the poor, the distribution of food (*'aish al-Hussain*) among the Shi'a in 'Ashura, the custom of slaughtering sheep to honour the visit of a celebrity, as well as the etiquette of hospitality which require, among other things, serving coffee and/or offering sweets – these rituals intend in various ways to establish strong bonds between participants. In Arab culture, sharing food rejuvenates kinship solidarity and seals peaceful agreements between fighting parties. It is a symbol of unity and common interest.

Wars and raids among Arab nomads, which often erupt over claims to land, wells or pasture, are brought to an end by treaties of reconciliation crowned by a meal that brings together the warring factions. 'There is salt between us' is an expression always said in reference to well established friendship ties. The Lebanese proverb, 'Feeding the mouth makes the eye shy,' is meant to explain how aggression can be mitigated by food offerings.

In all these occasions, the distance narrows between the interactors to a range of approximately half to one metre. Like laughing in public, sharing food, eating of the same dish or at the same table, suspends formality and compromises authority. It often happens at these occasions that some participants abuse the rather informal atmosphere by coming closer or moving farther away from other participants than they should. If they adopt a position at the wrong distance, their behaviour could be offensive. Hence the popular saying, 'Blessed is he who knows his limit and stands by it.' But many of us don't know our limits; we act in the presence of the emir as if we were the emir himself, following the verse:

O my neighbour! If you visit me you will
be the host and I will be the guest.

Given the tremendous changes in the economic and technological order, and the concomitant changes that have followed in the social order, it would be expected that all sorts of imbalanced confrontations would take place in the socializing fields. This is perhaps the reason that the host, in order to secure a minimal level of harmony, carefully selects his guests taking into account social differentiation and personal moods and temperaments. Those who do not match are left aside. In my home town in North Lebanon, people argue for hours about who should visit whom and who should invite whom. And it often happens that 'the crop never measures up to its estimate in the field': there is always something wrong with somebody's selected list of guests and something wrong with the way they are treated. Here lies the significance of protocol.

The protocol arrangement tries to put things in order according to prescribed rules and regulations recognized internationally. Within this zone, the participants are not bound sentimentally as in the intimate field, nor do they share common interests as in the socializing field; they interact to negotiate and exchange information. This mode of interaction is practised by diplomats, or between subordinates and their superiors in structured organizations such as the army, or between buyers and sellers in the market, or between beggars and passers-by in public places. Interactors here are strangers who have no previous knowledge of each other, and because of this they need a prescribed formula in which to conduct their encounters without causing embarrassment.

Within the protocol field, people interact within a distance of a yard or a metre, give or take a few inches. This type of interaction is temporary; it ends with the accomplishment of the objectives for which it was originally set. However, it is possible that the transient encounter may recur several times in which case the protocol field may develop into a social mode of interaction or even an intimate one. If it does, the interactors would then assume equivalent status.

The fourth field of interaction, the lecture type, is distinguished by persuasion and deliberate instructions. Within this field a person tries to convert others to his viewpoint; he is the speaker, and they the audience. To be able to talk to them as a collective group, he separates himself from their midst in a distance ranging between one and two metres or more. This mode of interaction is often practised by speakers in mosques, priests in churches, politicians from elevated platforms, teachers and lecturers in schools and universities, and leaders in organized protests. If the audience responds positively to the speaker's advances, he gives up his detached position and moves close to them, mixing freely in their midst. However, mixing with the audience as means of marshalling support, is an attempt to mobilize them for a specific course of action. For organizational purposes, the speaker keeps distance physically while he is simultaneously an active member of the group – this indeed is a primary quality of leadership.

In fact, when a speaker addresses an audience, however large, he does not address them as if they were a single body. He speaks to them through the few who respond favourably to the speech. While lecturing at the American University of Beirut, I always felt that I was speaking to a handful of students in a class of forty. Were it not for the presence of this small group who attentively followed the discussion, the job would have been boring. Should boredom strike a speaker, it instantaneously radiates to the audience.

Of course, one can be fooled by body language. A student may give the lecturer the impression that he is following the discussion word by word in the classroom while in fact his mind is set on his girlfriend at home. The reverse could also be true: a student may give the lecturer the impression that his mind is distracted elsewhere whereas in fact he follows the discussion *verbatim*.

Thus far, I have been dealing with four different but related spheres of interaction affecting social distance as if the interactors always have the privilege of choice, each according to his ambitions, plans and relationships. In fact, they don't. It frequently happens that we are trapped in situations imposed upon us by external circumstances. Such is the case in using an escalator, going to the movie or theatre, travelling by plane or train, or formally receiving congratulations or condolences on solemn occasions at weddings and funerals. In these situations, the interactors operate within narrow proximity to each other, but they lack the intimate bond that normally comes along with narrow distance. In these circumstances, many an interactor withdraws from the scene by walking to the top of the escalator, concentrating on reading a journal or a book, or looking down at the floor, thus avoiding conversation with people around him/her. In movies or theatres, people try to protect their privacy by seeking wider distances, leaving, whenever possible, an empty seat between themselves and the rest.

Sometimes, the right gesture is used in the wrong context. A person, for example, may rush to kiss you on the cheek pretending to be a friend or a member of the family whereas in reality you don't know who the hell he is. Contradictions of this sort often occur at weddings or funerals between people belonging to different social backgrounds. It is ironic that these contradictions take place at weddings and funerals, the very occasions that call for unity, collaboration and support. Ironic it may be, but it is understandable. Weddings, and more so funerals, open a new page in the relationships between people where customs and traditions supersede individual whims and moods. Traditions require that on such solemn occasions people forget their squabbles and lend support to each other, i.e. narrow the distance. In fact, some, especially politicians, take advantage of this ruling to mend their disputes with their enemies and competitors. Approaching people on such symbolically condensed rituals does not entail any negative implications, whereas in normal life it does. Take, for example, the case of making visits. Following a quarrel of some sort, people sever relationships and stop exchanging visits. However, after a lapse of time they might regret what happened and wish to resume relations. Their personal dignity and self-pride do not allow for immediate action; they await such occasions as weddings, funerals or sickness to visit their enemies and reconcile the conflict. In normal life, a visit of this order would undermine the person's dignity, honour and reputation. In times of grief or joy, the visit is *ipso facto* justified; hence, the reconciliation.

CHAPTER 9

The Strategy of Sitting

Where and how we sit defines our status, moods and attitudes and raises many questions and considerations pertaining to our image and self-image. As we walk into a public assembly for the first time, unless we are ushered into our seats, we pause and look around trying to identify a person we know who enjoys the same status as we do. If we find one, we normally opt to sit beside him/her. We hesitate to just take any seat lest we offend somebody or reflect negatively on our own image. In formal meetings, the seating order is arranged in advance according to rules of protocol; each participant takes the place already assigned to him/her. In the absence of protocol, the social order takes priority. Men of means, power and authority normally occupy the central place and beside them sit other celebrities; the closer the celebrities are to the central place, the higher the status. However, the central place is not a geometric equation or an architectural formula; the centre lies where the men of authority sit. In his book, *The Interpretation of the Great Qur'an*, Ibn Kathir writes:

The Prophet used to choose his seat haphazardly anywhere in the room, but wherever he sat that would be the centre. His companions used to sit around him each depending on his status. Al-Siddiq [the first caliph] used to sit on his right side, and 'Umar [the second caliph] on his left, and in front of him 'Uthman and 'Ali [the third and fourth caliphs respectively] because they were among those who were writing down the revelation.[1]

It was mentioned earlier that priority is given to the right side because the left is believed to be polluted. Arab Muslims avoid shaking hands, eating, drinking, and sometimes writing with the left hand. Many a left-handed student is forced by his tutor to use the right; the left belongs to the devil. A guest taking a cup of coffee with the left hand insults the host.

Some people go out of their way to honour their guests by offering them the central seat. This form of hospitality often takes place when the guest occupies a higher status and wields more power and authority than the host.

The act of sitting signifies authority. The Queen of Great Britain remains seated in her throne while receiving the cabinet and members of parliament; Arab emirs likewise receive their guests and visitors in the same fashion. Traditionally the Arabs did not use chairs or sofas; they sat crouched on the floor covered with carpets or mats; hence, the phrase 'crouched on the throne' meaning held it with firmness and authority. It is cited in the Qur'an, 'And God is settled on the throne';[2] 'settled' in this context implies sitting firmly or comfortably i.e. with authority. Authority is implicit in the word throne, the high platform.

Higher platforms, raising somebody higher than somebody else, always marks differentiation in status and authority. Just as sitting on higher or lower levels corresponds to gradation in rank, sitting at the same level signifies equality. No wonder that during elections candidates emphasize the principle of equality by mixing freely with their constituents listening attentively to their complaints and grievances. In Sufi circles, private religious meetings, scientific conferences, and in other assemblies governed by the principle of equality, the participants sit on the same level around the table.

Offering seats to people is a way of honouring them. The Qur'an states:

> O ye who believe! When you are told to make space in the councils [for others] do so. God will provide you with more space. And when you are told to leave your seats, do so. God will raise you up to [higher] ranks.[3]

In other words, offering seats to others does not diminish a person's status; it is an act of raising a person's rank in the eyes of God.

I have been dealing so far with sitting as if it were a unified, monolithic posture, which it is not. In Arab-Islamic culture, some sitting postures display power and authority, some generate comfort and rest, some cause aversion and disgust, and some are considered abhorrent. In the first instance, the body takes on a perpendicular posture in harmony with the seat, and the legs are kept tightly together in a parallel shape that covers the genitals (*figure 3*).

A person may seek comfort by slightly extending one leg and contracting the other; this is an acceptable posture that guarantees him a measure of comfort without offending others (*figure 4*).

But to sit in a chair with the upper part of the body twisted

Figure 3
Sitting displaying authority.

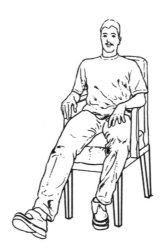

Figure 4
Sitting in a comfortable position without causing offence.

Figure 5
Aggressive mode of sitting.

in one direction and the lower part in another, with the legs open at an acute angle, thus displaying the genitals is considered disgusting. The person in this posture looks as if he is ready to make love (*figure 5*). Simultaneously, this posture exhibits domineering tendencies, aggressiveness and masculinity, which are somehow appreciated qualities for men in Arab culture. This is not surprising since sexual gestures explicitly overlap with dominance, as will be demonstrated later in some detail.

In the last instance, the abhorrent type, a person sinks in his chair receiving visitors while his legs are stretched over the office desk with the sole of his shoes facing those coming into the room. This posture, which is typically practised in America, makes Arabs squeamish. To them the shoes are

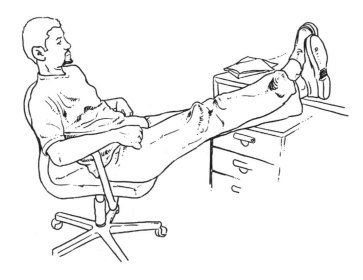

Figure 6
Abhorrent style of sitting.

polluted and cause pollution; therefore they should be taken off during prayer or upon entering the holy mosque, or even a house. I know an Arab student in America who changed his field of specialization because his professor repeatedly received him while sitting in this position (*figure 6*).

There is another dimension to the strategy of sitting which relates to its geometric designs – namely, the angles the interactors adopt towards each other. Before I deal with this question, I would like to distinguish between custom and habit. Custom is a social, public concern transmitted across generations, whereas habit is personal behaviour initially chosen at random, but which becomes entrenched with time by sheer repetition. For example, shaving or trimming one's beard is a custom, but starting from the right or the left side, or reversibly from the neck upward or vice versa is a habit. What is said about shaving can be generalized to other customs as well – marriage, worship, bathing or chasing women. Indeed, every form of behaviour has two faces, a public one recognized by custom and a private one practised by individuals. Within the public pattern, the individual selects the alternative that suit his moods and socio-economic background. Take, for example, prayer in Islam. Its general framework is known; it starts with ablution and ends in invocation, kneeling and bowing before the Almighty. In reality, however, no worshipper approaches prayer exactly like the other. While performing the ritual, some may be thinking of a commercial deal, some of their children and whether or not they will pass school exams, some of their parents and friends, or still of lovers and mistresses, and some focus on God and religion. Hence, the Qur'anic verse, 'There be no compulsion in religion'.[4] Religion is exoterically a sanction and esoterically a sacrament.

I have dealt with sitting so far as custom; in the following I shall deal with it as habit. In stable groups where people interact continuously in a routine fashion, participants tend to occupy the same seats repeatedly day after day. The repetition is not sustained by formal etiquette as much as by personal choice. It looks as if the seats we have chosen for the first time haphazardly at random become with time an integral part of the structure and dynamics of the group to which we belong – a habit.

Such habitual patterns seem to prevail mostly in stable groups which continue to interact among themselves for a lengthy period of time – family members, village communities, students in classrooms, worshippers in mosques and churches. While I was lecturing at the American University of Beirut and other universities, I noticed that students continue to sit in the same place they had chosen for the first time. Of course, the first choice might have been prompted by many factors: to be near friends, in the back corner near the window to watch passers-by, in the front seats to follow the discussion at a close distance, or at the back to have freedom of movement. Once a person makes the initial choice, he will be trapped by it, as if he is guided by a hidden electronic device.

This continued repetition of choice could not be explained physiologically by seeking comfort or sociologically by affirming status; more likely it is linked to a network of relationships and attitudes that the seating order generates within an interacting group. Such relationships and attitudes become manifest in what I like to call 'the architecture of sitting', the angles and distances that separate interactors.

I have already discussed the circular arrangement and the sense of equality and freedom of expression it creates between participants. Contrary to the circular shape there is the straight line having a 180° angle; this is the way people are lined up for prayer or military exercise, lacking both equality and freedom of expression. No wonder that the military have adopted the motto: 'Execute and then protest.'

However, between the circular arrangement and the straight line, there lie many postures each conveying a distinct meaning. If two interactors sit face to face around a table at an even level, they are in a negotiating position (*figure 7*). This is how equals negotiate. If any one of them seeks a raised platform, he/she is assuming a pre-eminent position, the master-apprentice relationship.

On the other hand, if they sit near one another at an acute angle, on two adjacent sides of the table, they take a mutually sympathetic position (*figure 8*). This is how lovers sit.

Figure 7
Sitting in a negotiating position.

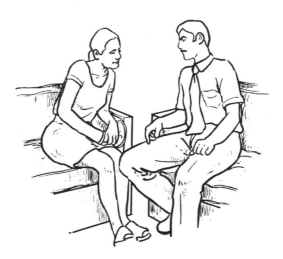

Figure 8
Sitting in a mutually sympathetic position.

Figure 9
Inviting the third interactor to participate in the process.

If a third person is present, one of two alternatives may take place, either they invite him/her to participate in the interactional process or they ignore him/her. If the two interactors invite the third to take part, they shift their faces and bodies, including the feet, towards him/her, as in *figure 9*.

If, for one reason or another, they opt to exclude him/her, they turn away their faces and bodies (*figure 10*). This last posture is summarized by the Arabic expression, 'Show me the breadth of your shoulders,' which literally means move out.

Early in my career when I was working on the etiquette of bargaining in the Middle East,[5] I noticed that these angles of interaction change with the stages of the bargaining epi-

Figure 10
Ignoring the third interactor.

sode. As soon as the buyer enters the shop, the seller, while welcoming him politely, leaves his chair and arranges to seat the buyer near him at an acute angle on the adjacent side of the desk (the position of mutual sympathy). The moment the seller feels that the buyer has relaxed and starts to bargain for price, he changes his position to meet the buyer face-to-face in a negotiating position. As a signal of possible failure, the buyer becomes somehow restless moving from one angle of interaction to another. If they fail to conclude a deal, the seller or the buyer each turns away his body and moves on, a gesture to terminate the episode. If they succeed, the seller would walk the buyer to the front door and beyond.

These angles of interaction remain constant irrespective

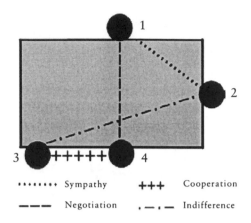

••••••• Sympathy	+++ Cooperation
——— Negotiation	, — , — Indifference

Figure 11
The angles of interaction between people sitting around a table.

of the size of the group. In other words, people interact in (1) a mutually sympathetic position, (2) a negotiating position, (3) a cooperating position, or (4) with indifference and withdrawal. *Figure 11* illustrates these varied dimensions graphically.

These angles of interaction constitute an implicit, silent language that not only shows the quality of relationships between people, but could simultaneously be used to induce such relationships. We have just seen how the buyer and seller change these angles concomitantly with the stages of development of the bargaining episode. Likewise, if you want to generate an atmosphere of trust and sympathy you take the sympathetic position. By contrast, if you want to withdraw you take the indifferent position. Here lies the ability of people to read the silent messages others display through body language of this sort.

It must be stressed at this point that these angles of interaction do not occur in isolation; they are often accompanied by other detectable gestures and body movements. The mutually sympathetic position, for example, is often accompanied by relaxed facial expressions, widening the eyes, straight short smiles, and subtle body inclinations towards the other interactor. Contrarily, the indifferent position is often accompanied by tense facial expressions, narrowing the eyes, stiff lips, and moving the body away from the other interactor. The negotiating position, on the other hand, is accompanied by initially putting on a poker face which may shift later from one gesture to another depending upon the level of progress made. Trying to persuade the other partner, negotiators may manipulate different gestures continuously oscillating between smiling and firmness, sarcasm and seriousness, emphasis and hesitation, boredom and attentiveness, anger and contentment.

In negotiating episodes, a person may move from one position or mood to its opposite in a very short while depending upon the prevailing circumstances. Businessmen seem to resort to the use of such tactics more often than other professions such as teachers or medical doctors. Consider the following anecdote.

In 1982 I was visiting a businessman in his office in Beirut and while we were exchanging news and jokes about the Lebanese war, his private telephone rang. He took the receiver and after a while he frowned with signs of anger filling his face, and started scolding the other fellow on the line using the harshest words possible. I had never seen him behaving in such a fury. In a moment he changed from a calm, cool person to a predator looking for prey.

Suddenly, in a split of a second, he put the telephone aside, turned to me and with a big smile said, 'How do you like your coffee sweet, medium or bitter?' At that point I had no choice, 'Sweet,' I said, although I like it bitter.

By shifting moods from one extreme to another, from calmness to rebelliousness and vice versa, businessmen and politicians try to mould events to their own liking.

CHAPTER 10

Sexual Gestures and Body Movements

Whenever I mention to a colleague or a friend that I am working on body language, they would giggle and say, 'Aha! Sex, sex and then sex,' as if the total sphere of body language focuses on nothing other than sex. Well, if not all, a great part of it does. There is hardly a gesture or body movement with a clear explicit meaning that does not directly or indirectly carry a sexual connotation, or move either partly or totally through sexual drives. The French expression, 'cherchez la femme,' does not only explain the role women play in causing family conflicts and wars, but also in the choice of food, drink and clothes; in the appreciation of art, poetry and literature; or in various displays of body charms. In all these fields, women affect the outcome and mould its contents.

Not only do sexual gestures and body movements recur more often than others in body language, but they seem to frequently overlap with gestures signifying control, aggression, violence or dominance. In Arab-Islamic culture, making love is metaphorically understood to be an act of 'tearing', 'severing', 'conquest' and 'plowing' – all indicating rupture in the virginity membrane.[1]

Figure 12
The legs in a sexually arousing position.

How similar are the worlds of man and animal! Just as a cock spreads out its tail, extends its wings, stretches its neck, and raises its head in preparation to mount the hen, so do men to charm women. On beaches and verandahs young men, at the sight of girls, blow up their chests, stretch their necks upward, display their biceps, and stand up straight ready for the sexual act. Should they wish to approach girls in public places or private parties, they almost involuntarily mend their clothes, fix their neckties, comb their hair, and straighten their jackets.

In their turn, girls try to charm boys by 'stealing an eye catch' (this is a literal translation from Arabic), using ornaments or perfume, or walking with the buttocks moving gently right and left. Very often, they try to win attention with a subtle wink, a delicate hand or leg movement; or gently pushing their hair backward to expose the face or part of it, and raise the sleeves to show the skin's softness and colour. The stereotype men have of women, creatures with many tricks, often refers to the use of these tactics.

Sexual gestures and body movements operate positively or negatively in various fields of interaction. They operate to express love and sacrifice – we all know the heart wounded by the spear of love – or contradictorily to deliver insults or threats. Freudian psychology will appreciate this: every movement or gesture performed by hand, leg, foot or finger which might take roughly a penis shape, or the shape of a hole or cavity that resembles the vagina carries with it a sexual connotation. In this sphere, the tongue and the limbs seem to be the most active organs. It is interesting to note that the Qur'an has referred to body language in the following words:

> On the day [of Judgment] when their tongues, their hands, and their legs will bear witness against them as to their actions.[2]

As instruments of expression, the legs, being linked to the unconscious and move in accordance with it, are perhaps more reliable indicators than the hands. People seem to be more spontaneous and less conscious of the movements they make with their legs than their hands.[3] This difference can be traced to its physiological roots whereby the part of the brain that controls the hands is much more complex than the one controlling the legs.[4]

Leg gestures and movements may take various positions, each conveying a special meaning. Some positions are sexually arousing. In an arousing position, the legs are slightly open on the genitalia at an acute angle (*figure 12*), and the

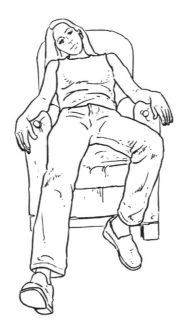

Figure 13
The feet in a sexually arousing position.

feet take the shape of a perpendicular or an obtuse angle with the tip of one foot pointing towards the other interactors while the second lies within the stretch of his body (*figure 13*). In this position, it looks as if one is trying to embrace the other by using the legs instead of the hands. Here, the two interactors are fully aware of each other's positions.

In the unconscious movements of legs and feet, the dress, however long, dark or baggy, will not conceal the messages transmitted through body language. The dress may mask the body and veil the face, but will not hide the movements and positions of the legs and the feet, or the general direction of

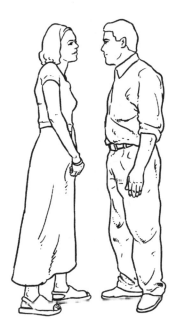

Figure 14
The body in a sexually attractive position.

the body as a whole. In the sexually attractive position, the body as a whole opens and leans towards the other person; the eyes engulf him with passion; the feet gently tap the floor inviting him to come closer *(figure 14)*.

Addressing women, the Qur'an says:

[They] should not strike their feet in order to draw attention to their ornaments.[5]

In explaining this verse, Ibn Kathir says:

Figure 15
Legs adjoined in a sexually indifferent position.

In the pre-Islamic days, the days of ignorance, women used to walk in public streets wearing a rattling bracelet at the ankles. In order to draw attention, they used to tap the floor with their feet and the bracelet would rattle. God then instructed women believers to stop doing this.[6]

In modern times, many girls and boys exhibit their mutual attraction by using clear sexual gestures, a privilege that had not been practised in traditional Islamic communities. These gestures include walking together with crossed fingers, touching shoulders, holding necks, or bringing their bodies together. It must be said, however, that few people in Arab-Islamic culture use these gestures in public; many more use them at private parties or enclaves such as palm tree parties

Figure 16
Legs and arms in a locked position.

to which only the very select are invited, or in secluded beaches where membership is restricted to exclusive families.

Of course, most significant of all is kissing which is universally practised in private as a prelude to intercourse. In public, it is often done in western countries or western oriented cultures such as Australia and New Zealand. In the Middle East, I have seen it done only at foreign university campuses.

These sexually exciting or attractive gestures are counterbalanced by indifferent postures. In these postures, the legs adjoin in a parallel way from the rumps to the feet, and the whole body closes on itself; in a sitting order, the person sits upright at a perpendicular angle to the chair (*figure 15*). This posture is so dull sexually that it is often practised in formal negotiations.

Figure 17
Legs crossed.

It is also possible to express sexual indifference by lock-ing or crossing the legs and the arms. In either case the *farj* is covered. However, men tend to practice the crossed position more often than women who are subject to modesty con-straints. Unlike the locked position (*figure 16*), the crossed one (*figure 17*) may, in its extreme form, expose the inner part of the *farj*.

Roughly speaking, sexual gestures and body movements seem to focus mainly on the ways the legs are used to either open or close on the *farj*. And it makes no difference whether this opening or closing occurs through adjoining, locking or crossing the legs while sitting or standing. Here lies the dif-ference between men and women. Whereas men underline an aggressive attitude, masculinity, and the readiness to take initiative by opening slightly on the *farj*, women, by contrast, highlight their concern with modesty and the protection of family honour by closing on it.

No doubt, the discrepancy between men and women is occasioned by the double standards prevailing in Arab-Islamic culture. Whereas women are expected to contain and restrain their sexuality, men brag about their exploits. Obviously women's sexual expectations are culturally incongruous with men's exploits. Hence the old profession, prostitution, which, while allowing men to cherish their exploits, makes it possible for women to live up to the cultural dictum.

The overlap or correspondence between sexual gestures and body movements, on the one hand, and those implying power, dominance, aggression, violence and authority, on the other, is striking. A considerable number of documentaries on animals and birds in the wild have shown that when submitting to the more powerful and dominant, the weaker, male and female, assume a sexual posture.

In the same vein, just as women stare at the floor and bend their heads slightly forward to express acceptance of their husbands' dominance and sexual advances, so do men before their masters. However, the same gestures in this context are interpreted differently: whereas women express modesty, propriety and good upbringing in displaying these gestures, men express subservience. In other words, what appears to be an act of modesty for women is construed to be an act of subservience for men.

The overlap between sex and dominance is also carried out in more subtle ways using the eyes. Given men's Arab dress and women's Islamic dress, the eye becomes the most visibly active vehicle of communication in body language.

Many love songs, expressions and popular wit and wisdom speak of the various gestures the eye can deliver: to establish dialogue or favourable communication by using the eyes, which I shall call 'eye-dialogue' (*hiwar al-'uyun*), staring eyes (*tahdiq*), the angry eye, the evil eye, the jealous eye. Eye-dialogue occurs when two people meet for the first time and try to explore each other's inner motives. It is a dialogue between equals subject to the principle of 'structured reciprocity' i.e., the exchange takes place in kind and degree. It is often characterized by short but repeated, neutral and inoffensive glances. It is so neutral that it is sometimes referred to as 'stealing a glance'.

Unlike eye-dialogue, eye-staring is subject to the law of unstructured reciprocity; it often takes place between non-equals whereby the strong stares at the weak who are expected to lower their gaze. If the weak stare back they are challenging the authority of the strong. In pre-Islamic poetry, a famous verse states:

Lower your gaze since you are from the Numair tribe;
You have not yet reached the glory of Ka'b or Kulaib.

It is all a matter of self-perception, the attempt to define one's status *vis-à-vis* other interactors. In this process, all kinds of contradictions and incongruities may emerge. If you perceive yourself as being or wanting to be equal to the other person, you try to look at him/her in a manner implying dialogue. If he/she rejects your advance, he/she stares at you with anger which is often accompanied by frowning eyebrows and contracting pupils, stiff lips, and constrained facial expressions.

The evil eye and the jealous eye belong to the world of

black magic and witchcraft. Acting independently of the person who possesses them, they hit the beautiful, the unique and the marvellous – a healthy child, a successful business-man, a handsome male, a pretty female, a fat sheep, a strong horse, a fertile apple tree, or a taxi Mercedes car. And to ward off the evil eye, the person must protect himself/herself by wearing an amulet. While Christians wear the cross, the fish, or a variety of icons symbolizing Christ, the Virgin Mary, or any of the church saints, Muslims wear the cres-cent, or any of the Qur'anic verses especially the 'Chair' verse. The Shi'a Muslims use for this purpose the Palm of Abu Fadl al-'Abbas who was able to kill hundreds of the Umayyad's troops in the famous battle of Karbala.

Human beings, especially infants, and animals are also protected by blue beads on the basis that 'like begets like': the evil eye is believed to be blue and therefore could be dis-tracted by blue beads. Objects such as trees, vegetable gardens or taxi Mercedes cars are often protected by making them look ugly; this is done by having old rotten shoes and empty egg shells hung onto them.

No where is the correspondence between sex and domi-nance more explicitly visible than in finger gestures and hand movements. Creativity in this sphere of interaction is very impressive. In this respect, the middle finger is perhaps the most active of all. It signifies 'fucking' or 'screwing' if it, alone, is stretched vertically upward while the rest of the fin-gers close on the palm. In this position, it stands for the penis and the palm for the body (figure 18).

Should the finger be pointed horizontally at a particular person, it would convey an aggressive mood often accompa-nied by abusive language such as threatening to fuck the opponent's mother and sisters. Should it be pointed verti-cally downward instead of upward, it would signify an

Figure 18
Gesture implying fucking.

Figure 19
The fucking gesture in Britain.

already accomplished victory or distinction; it is done out of spite. In other words, to conquer is to fuck. After all, making love can be an act of conquest.

With some slight modification, the use of fingers in a gesture suggestive of sex is widespread. In Great Britain, for example, 'fucking' is expressed by raising the middle finger and the index in a 'V' shape with the back of the palm pointed towards the other person (*figure 19*). It is the same sign for victory, but instead of turning the face of the palm towards the others, it is turned towards oneself. In other words, you are the victorious and the other party is the vanquished.

It is also possible to convey the same meaning, fucking and victory, by moving the hand and the fist back and forth horizontally at a perpendicular angle to the body (*figure 20*). In this gesture, the hand would stand for the penis and the fist for its tip.

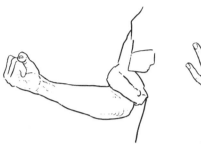 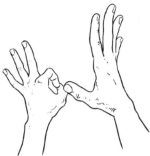

Figure 20
The use of the fist to express
sexual potency.

Figure 21
Gesture implying intercourse and
dominance.

A similar meaning is also conveyed by opening a hole-like circle in the left hand, which is done by bringing the tips of the index and the thumb together, and then covering the hole speedily with the palm of the left hand. This gesture signifies both intercourse and dominance (*figure 21*).

Parallel to this gesture is an inverted victory sign (*figure 22*) facing downward instead of upward.[7] The sign thus created stands for 'mounting' which again carries at once a sexual and a dominant connotation. In the sense of dominance, the analogy is made in reference to the plowing board that keeps the two bulls together in tilling the soil. One of the meanings of 'plowing' in Arabic is intercourse.

There remains a final gesture that reflects the overlap between sex and dominance and that is for a person to gently pinch, often using the index and the thumb, someone's cheek. Just as a mother may pinch her child to show affection and implicit superiority, the strong may thus pinch the weak to underline simultaneously their affection and dominance (*figure 23*). The weak never reciprocate.

Figure 22
The inverted victory
sign; the act of
'plowing'.

Figure 23
Pinching the cheek
affectionately, but with
dominance.

The question is: how does this overlap between sex and dominance in body language affect the concept of love and love relationships?

CHAPTER 11

I Am 'Antara and She Loves Me

The overlap between sex and dominance in Arab-Islamic culture has given rise to a very special way of defining love and love relationships. I am calling this special definition and relationship the 'Antara Complex' i.e. love as one-way traffic; it is the property of women, not men. 'Antara bin Shaddad al-'Absi is a legendary hero who combined military prowess with passionate poetry. As a fighter in battle no body could surpass his courage; he says of himself:

> When the strongest of men fearing my might retreat,
> Long territories shrink to metres and yards.

Yet, he is a poet – and a warrior poet is a rare thing – who says of his lover 'Abla:

> Truthfully I wish, by God, I could cure you
> From the sickness of my love.

In other words, she loves him intensely to the extent of being 'sick', which implies the height of love. He only wishes he could cure her – the implication being he could not.[1]

Many Arabs hold 'Antara in great esteem; to them he is

the ideal man. Robust men do not fall for what is often referred to as women's tricks and traps, meaning love. The
association between women's tricks, traps and love is as ancient as the Old Testament. In Genesis, it was Eve who was
tricked by the serpent to tempt Adam to eat the fruit of the
tree of knowledge, thus disobeying God's instructions. As a
result, God punished the serpent by making it eat dust and
crawl on its belly, punished Eve by increasing the pain of her
labour and designating man [Adam] as her master, and punished Adam by expelling him from the Garden of Eden and
making him earn his bread by sweat; 'dust you are and to
dust you shall return'.[2]

The same anecdote occurs in the Qur'an with some mild
modifications. Instead of the serpent, it was Satan who
tricked 'Adam and his wife' to eat from the 'tree of eternity'.[3]
At once, they saw their nakedness as a source of shame. They
were expelled from the Garden to live 'with enmity one to
another'.[4]

Women in Arab-Islamic culture are believed to be capable of casting nets and setting traps: they 'fish' and 'hunt'
for husbands. There prevails the belief that love is an instrument – the line, the hook and the bait – women use to catch
men. Finding a husband is thought to depend on sheer luck
in a complicated lottery, much like fishermen fishing in the
sea. No wonder that men in their circles refer to marriage as
'the golden cage'; it is a 'cage' by virtue of being trapped,
and 'golden' because of the comfort it brings.

> And He created for you mates, that ye may dwell in tran-
> quillity with them . . .[5]

This suggests that a woman's love is simply a measure of her ability to deal with the world of men. Therefore, a woman loving a man is fair and acceptable behaviour that conforms to customs and religious traditions.

> We have created them [women] in a special way for the believers, and made them virgins, of equal age [to their husbands] and lovers of their husbands.[6]

Virgins are preferred in marriage; their dower is always higher than non-virgins. Wives are preferred to be of more or less equivalent age to their husbands. In my research on the suburbs of Beirut, I found that there is a narrower age gap between husbands and wives among Muslims than Christians.[7] Wives who sexually desire their husbands out of love and affection are also a distinguished group;[8] they are known as 'urub.[9] A well-authenticated hadith affirms: 'A woman is contracted in marriage for her looks, wealth, or noble origin.'

For women to be in love with their husbands is only one of many duties and responsibilities towards him. The bulk of these duties focus on obedience in sexual and non-sexual matters, loyalty, and adornment – adornment only for the husband. It is cited in a hadith:

> I tell you about your wives who are promised a place in Heaven: the loyal, the child-bearing and the forgiving. The one who would come back to you, even after you hurt her, and say: 'I shall not close my eyes [sleep] until you are content.'[10]

By contrast, the duties of a husband towards his wife focus on economic support, equity and kind treatment.[11]

Live with them [the wives] on a footing of kindness and equity [between co-wives]. If ye take a dislike to them it may be that ye dislike a thing and God brings about through it a great deal of good.[12]

Men are requested to deal kindly with their wives and to sustain their livelihood, not to fall in love or to admire their character and beauty. True, man and wife are equal in creation, but within this framework men are a 'degree' [of priority] ahead of women:

And women shall have rights similar to the rights against them, according to [the principle of] equity. But men have a degree [of advantage] over them.[13]

This Qur'anic verse is then followed by another that explains the meaning of degree rather clearly:

Men have priority over women because God has given them more strength and [the duty] to support women from their wealth.[14]

The 'degree' then is one of responsibility to support, protect and guard women, not one of love and affection. If it happens that a man falls in love with a woman, he will be designated by his love: such is the case of Majnun Laila, literally meaning Laila's Madman; his nickname becomes Laila by virtue of his love for her.

Whereas a woman's love reflects upon her ability to deal with the world of men, men's love is an act of fantasy and madness. This understanding of men's love can be best illustrated in the famous works of the Damascene poet Nizar

Qabbani who earned for himself the nickname women's poet:

> Because of the intensity of my love [for her],
> I cry like a madman.[15]

> Now I am passing through the moments
> Of my 'great madness'.
> Should you fail to take advantage of my madness,
> The joy of your life will be lost.[16]

Qabbani then tries to find synonyms for 'the moments of great madness', which came to be 'the shining madness',[17] 'the colossal madness,'[18] 'the bright madness'[19] – all referring to sexual love. The same meaning recurs in some of his other works:

> At night, when I mount the train of madness,
> And as long as you are with me,
> I don't care for what is already
> Passed or what will be.[20]

> I know not what is flowing through my inner soul,
> But I am glad to move from madness to madness,
> And then madness.[21]

> My love!
> Because the one who loves in my city is mad,
> I decided to specialize in poetry and madness.[22]

> Enhance my love abundantly
> Oh! the most beautiful tune of my madness.[23]

What shall we call the love that pierces our body
Like a knife?
Shall we call it pain, or shall we call it madness.[24]

Unlike sexual love which is thought to be an act of madness, love for the tribe, the country and the nation, and the readiness to sacrifice one's self for them is an act of heroism and a symbol of martyrdom. This again is an 'Antara-like glorious stand.

However, through a process of psychological substitution, sexual love combines with love for nations to transform countries into lovers, darlings and sweethearts. Many Arab writers refer to their countries in such metaphors: 'My darling', 'our raped land', '[the occupiers] have uncovered her naked body,' 'fucked her honour' – these and many other phrases of this order, which clearly carry sexual connotations, are said of Palestine, the land occupied by Israel today.

Likewise, in an emotive eulogy on Beirut titled 'Beirut the Destruction' Nizar Qabbani writes:

Oh! My only woman amongst millions of females.[25]

They cut short your long beautiful hair;
They robbed you of time and
Of your beautiful age.[26]

I didn't care whether you were naked or half naked!
I didn't care who shared your room or your bed!
The greatest of all concerns
Is to discover that I still love you.[27]

At this stage, it is important to distinguish between two

sets of love: sexual and heroic love, on the one hand, and sexual love and love-making (intercourse), on the other. Sexual love is the property of women; they are the *'urub*, the wives who sexually desire their husbands out of love and devotion. There is no word parallel to *'urub* that describes men who sexually desire their wives out of love and devotion. It is heroic love, the 'Antara way, which is the property of men, as manifested in the defence of family honour, the tribe, the nation, and the country. Women are the honour of men, which carries with it the responsibility to protect and provide for them, but at the same time be responsible for their behaviour. A misbehaving woman soils the honour of her father and brother in particular. What is called 'honour crime' is for a husband or a brother to murder a sexually loose daughter or sister.

In this context, the honour group refers to mothers and sisters, and is sometimes extended to encompass the incest group, the women that a man is forbidden to marry: sisters and brother's daughters, mother's and father's daughters, and other very close relations.

From an ideal viewpoint, the desired state of affairs is that women are expected to love, and men make love. Much like the defence of the group or the country, making love is treated as an act of heroism highly cherished by people. Nowhere is this belief better recognized than in what is known in Arab-Islamic culture as the 'night of penetration' often referred to in foreign sources as the 'virginity test'.

In Arab-Islamic culture, marriage passes through two formal stages: signing the marriage contract, and the consummation of marriage. In the first stage, the bride and the groom and their respective guardians come to a formal agreement about the dower and the manner of its payment. The agreement seals the marriage in the sense that the spouses become legally married. But the consummation of marriage comes later; the lapse of time between the two stages may vary between one month and a year or more. The consummation of marriage, which is known as 'the night of penetration', is celebrated with great joy: eating, dancing and singing. When the newly-wed couple retreat to sleep late at night, the parents and their guests wait to see blood stains displayed on a white cloth as a testimony to the bride's virginity. Affirming the bride's virginity, which indicates her good upbringing as well as the manliness of the groom, the crowd waiting outside welcome the news with sighs of relief and joy.

In brief, for a man to be loved, an object of women's love, marks the height of manliness; but to fall in love is a sign of weakness and effeminate behaviour. As teenagers we used to sing:

If you are beset by love spit on yourself;
I did and wish you the same.

The role a man plays in a love relationship is to acquire the manly personality traits; to present himself as the object of women's love. In other words, his role is self-contained; like 'Antara, he is ready to cure her from the sickness of his love. These images are shown in the love poetry of classical figures such as 'Antara, 'Amr Ibn Kulthum or 'Ūmar bin Abi-Rabi'a; their poetry focuses on the exploits of men and the physical beauty of women. Whereas male lovers are described as the warriors, the pillagers, the conquerors, the courageous knights, the masters of horsemanship, the handlers of swords and spears, the oppressors of the enemy; the female lovers are described as having long sleek necks, rosy cheeks, pearly teeth, lustrous eyes, and good upbringing.

A number of factors – the stereotypes held about women of being fast to reach orgasm; the belief that love is a woman's property which she uses to trap men; the cultural dictum implying that the honour of men lies in women's sexual behaviour and therefore women have to be watched, protected and guarded – these factors, among others, make any gesture or body movement exchanged across the gender line sexually loaded. Any touch, a shoulder tap, a wink, a glance, or a handshake; any physical contact, physical closeness, or exchange of smiles; any favourable reaction to jokes or opinions; any swinging walk, or finger and hand gesture to attract attention – any one of these if exchanged between men and women acquires a sexual connotation.

To avoid these delicate, culturally sensitive and sexually suggestive encounters, the world of men is segregated from the women's, especially in public places: markets, schools, universities, hospitals, movies. Veiling and wearing the long dark gown that covers the whole body is again another form of segregation. In some traditional circles, women's fashionable dress, such as the *burqu'* that stretches the nose out of proportion to the face or the use of dark colours are meant to publicize ugliness rather than announce beauty.

Culture has its own logic. Because of the segregation of the sexes, the mother and sister play the major role in selecting brides for sons and brothers. I was told by a *mulla* in Bahrain that once the decision is taken to approach a girl as a potential bride for a brother, his sister befriends her to run several tests. The sister pinches the potential bride in the back to test for temperament, kisses her on the mouth to test for smell, and tries to see her naked body to observe skin colour and general physique.[28] Her findings are then reported to the brother; the final decision is his.

It is because of this segregation that many an Arab, upon meeting a female, exhibits various signs of hesitation and sometimes embarrassment. These signs include blushing, stammering, lowered voices, and avoidance of face-to-face interaction by looking at the floor or the sky. However, soon as the interactors get acquainted with one another, these signs disappear.

Hesitation and embarrassment may harm marriage relationships particularly in the early stages, and may even lead to divorce. Upon checking the court records in Bahrain, I found that about one in every three divorces were filed within one year of marriage; not all of them ended in actual divorce. The newly-wed couple needed time to get to know and then adapt to each other's ways.

Marriage appears to pass through three stages: (1) mutual admiration, (2) tug of war and (3) mutual avoidance of areas of conflict. In the first stage, which lasts from the time they get acquainted till marriage, whatever he or she says and does is wonderful and marvellous; tolerance and appreciation of each other's ways is at its best. Once they get married they begin the second stage, tug of war; here each spouse tries to define his or her responsibilities within the household. What you do during the first week of marriage is likely to remain your domain of action for a long period of time. If you shop for food, take care of the garden, wash the dishes, serve drinks to guests, you may continue doing these until further notice.

Jokes always carry a sense of seriousness. A joke about the tug of war stage tells of a cat that disobeyed her newly-wed master. As he drew the cane to punish the cat, and that was within two weeks of his marriage, the bride turned to him and said, 'You should have done this on the first night.'

This anecdote, which is repeatedly told in many Arab countries with some mild variations, is meant to show the importance of the early days of marriage for the mutual adjustment of the newly-weds. In Bahrain the bride stays for about one month in her mother's house after marriage to learn the rules of adjustment.

However, the tug-of-war stage may be concluded in a short while or may last for a long time. When it ends, if it ends, the couple have learned how to mutually avoid areas of conflict. This avoidance marks a successful, favourable pattern of adjustment; the lack of it may cause divorce. In other words, adjustment between spouses is attained negatively by avoiding conflict rather than positively by agreement or unity of purpose. Therefore, to say, as many Arab men do, that he married her young in order to mould her to his ways and style of life is simply another angle of the 'Antara complex.

CHAPTER 12

Auxiliary Gestures and Body Movements

What distinguishes the auxiliary gestures and body movements from other forms of body language is the fact that, like auxiliary verbs, they do not carry any meaning on their own; they acquire meaning as long as they accompany the spoken word. Take, for example, the meanings implied in the index finger raised, alone, upward while the other fingers are touching the palm (*figure 24*). This gesture may mean one, the first, or number one; an act of threatening, scolding or punishing; a way of displaying seriousness; or still asking for permission to talk in class or any other assembly. Which one of these meanings is intended can be recognized only if the spoken words accompanying it are taken into account. This is unlike the 'V' sign for victory that carries its meaning regardless, or, for that matter, the middle finger raised upward, meaning fucking or screwing. In general, these auxiliary gestures are often used either as symbols of the spoken word or to express a wide range of moods and temperaments: joy and anger, love and hatred, threat and fear, thrift and generosity, strength and weakness, alertness and boredom, praise and insult, conquest and submission, success and failure, beauty and ugliness, certainty and suspicion. I shall

Figure 24
The meanings of the index finger raised
upward.

discuss first the gestures that signify love and fear, alertness
and boredom; and then deal with other gestures all of which
are characterized by what I call 'the complex of highness'
i.e. the state of being higher.

Unlike sexual gestures and body movements which em-
ploy mainly the limbs, the auxiliary gestures for love and
fear engage in addition the eye and the mouth, and then the
heart, the pulse and the breath. In love situations, including
joyful and relaxed moods, the eye widens, the pupil dilates,
the breath shortens, the facial expressions ease with a straight
broad smile. Parenthetically, women may express loving
moods by blushing or looking downward at the floor; both
gestures signify shyness which in Arab culture is an appreciated quality in women. As mentioned earlier, the same
gestures indicate a subservient position among men.

In all cultures the eyes are considered a measure of beauty,
and broad, wide eyes a symbol of it. This applies to both
human beings and animals. The gazelle has always been a
focus of praise in Arab poetry for its wide eyes. It is cited in

the Qur'an: 'And we married them [the believers] to women with broad and lustrous eyes'.[1]

In situations of hatred and anger, on the other hand, these gestures assume the opposite form. The pupil contracts, facial expressions become tense; the wide, straight smile disappears, and there comes instead a slanted smile showing sarcasm and a lack of seriousness.

Physiologically, it is curious to note that the same conditions that arise in loving moods seem to emerge in situations of fear. In love or in fear, the heart beats faster, the pulse increases its intensity, blood pressure rises, the mind accelerates and the skin becomes more sensitive. Any touch between lovers may excite them sexually, irrespective of whether or not the touch falls on a sensitive organ such as the neck, the ear, the penis or the clitoris. Male lovers may experience an erection while talking to their girlfriends over the telephone.

During his day-to-day interaction with others, a person goes through a whole variety of experiences; some stick in the mind, others fade away. Of course, there are a number of external factors that affect the scale of attentiveness: private interests and personal whims, the quality of the speaker's voice, the standard of speech and the level of maturity, the background of the audience, even weather conditions. Some people are so insensitive to the moods of the audience that they continue talking irrespective of the other's response. Being self-indulgent, they do not suit a number of professions – diplomats, medical doctors, lawyers, judges and the like, that require a good knowledge of how to read the moods of others. Yet, there are those who speak only if they are listened to; they know how to read body language. As a matter of fact, to be a good speaker one has to be a good reader of body language.

Figure 25
Alert, attentive position.

It is not easy to describe precisely the gestures and body movements that imply alertness or boredom; in this area of interaction people are good actors. Some audiences look at the speaker with relaxed expressions and agreeable smiles giving the impression that they follow him/her word by word, whereas in fact their minds are elsewhere. This brand of people are good actors and bad listeners. For one reason or another, all of us wear masks during the process of interaction, which may be thick or thin depending upon the level of intimacy prevailing within the interacting group: the stronger the intimate bond, the thinner the mask; the weaker the intimacy, the thicker the bond. Frankness and transparency

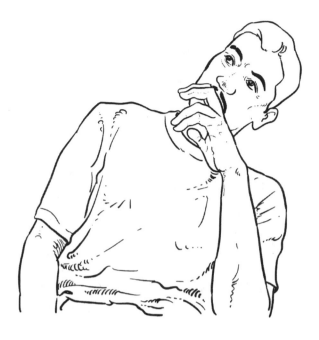

Figure 26
Posture indicating boredom.

indicate closeness and sympathy; concealment occasions withdrawal.

True, it is not easy to describe gestures that imply alertness or boredom, but in general it is not an impossible task. Very often concentration and alertness are accompanied by a slight bending of the head with a firm but unobtrusive smile. The body and the arms take on an open position, with the eyes gently cast on the speaker (*figure 25*).

Boredom, on the other hand, is expressed by inclining the head sideways to the right or the left, supported by the hand or the fingers accompanied with a slanted smile. In this position, the mouth tilts in one direction, sometimes towards the left, sometimes towards the right; the eyes move up and down, or sideways, deliberately avoiding the speaker (*figure 26*).

Some people express boredom in a very direct, blunt way by occupying themselves with activities that do not relate in one way or another to the point of discussion. Such is the case with a person who chooses to read a book or a newspaper during a lecture, or who, during a conversation, looks to the horizon or the sky while playing with his fingers, dusting his suit, or fixing his necktie.

There remains one group of gestures and body movements marked by 'the complex of highness.' It is a complex in two senses: (1) culturally, it prevails in a multitude of behaviours and (2) psychologically, people are obsessed with it. We say 'higher' for a person who is higher in status, more advanced in age, class, office, wealth or reputation in society. I have already alluded to the fact that the higher in status are known by the upper parts of the body: they are the eyes, the heads and the faces of society. The same principle is observed in the strategy of sitting discussed in *Chapter 10* as well as in a number of gestures and body movements.

As a rule of thumb, gestures and body movements that require lifting the head, the hands, the eyes, the brows or any other organ upward tend to indicate desirable qualities: strength, generosity, beauty, success, certainty. By contrast, downward gestures and movements often signify undesirable qualities: weakness, stinginess, ugliness, failure, suspicion.

A person expresses strength by raising his fist or index finger upward and then lifting the entire hand at a perpendicular angle upward. In this position, the hand is held parallel to the body as if the person concerned is displaying

Figure 27
Gesture implying strength.

his biceps (*figure 27*). Some people may choose to express strength by pushing the fist forward and backward in a straight line at a perpendicular angle to the body, which mimics ejaculation. This is not surprising since intercourse may be considered an act of dominance and conquest. However, these gestures do not occur in isolation; they are often accompanied by raising the head upward and straightening the body which together shows self-confidence and self-pride.

It is also possible to use these two gestures to express success, distinction or self-congratulation. In this sense, they resemble playing with one's hair, continuously fixing one's

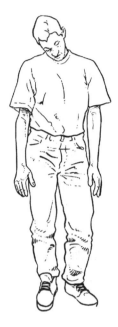

Figure 28
Gesture implying weakness and failure.

beard or moustache, or rubbing one palm against the other. People use these gestures to congratulate themselves on what they consider a remarkable achievement. The fact that many people perform these gestures when they are alone reinforces this interpretation. A good example of this would be a writer or an artist who performs these gestures-and movements upon creating something new that has never been done before. Or like a tennis player who pushes his fist forward and backward upon scoring an unexpected strike.

By contrast, gestures and body movements that express weakness and failure are performed in a reversed order i.e.

Figure 29
The gesture for begging.

by bending the head sideways while keeping the fingers open, and the hands lowered downward parallel to the body (*figure 28*). It is also possible to express weakness by opening the palms and then raising them slightly towards the sky, with the head bent forward to one side, as if the person is in a mood of worship. Man before God is weak. The open palm indicates readiness to be straightforwardly frank, and frankness is often, not always, a measure of weakness.

The open palm joined to a hand extended forward with the head inclined to one side signifies begging (*figure 29*). Strange enough, the same gesture with the hand raised a little

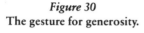

Figure 30
The gesture for generosity.

Figure 31
The gesture for stinginess.

higher comes to signify generosity. Except that in this case, the head would be raised upward and the body takes on a straight position (*figure 30*). It is said of a generous person that he/she have an open hand (palm) extended to the needy. On the other hand, stinginess is conveyed by closing the fingers against the palm, and then moving the hand downwards (*figure 31*).

Apparently, the angle the hand assumes in relation to the body, and the direction the open palm takes modify the meaning. If the hand is fully extended and raised to the level of the head, and the palm is opened towards the horizon, as if the person is greeting a crowd; this indicates leadership (*figure 32*). The statues of the late strong Syrian leader, President Hafiz al-Assad, erected on the motorway between the two cities of Homs and Damascus, or one of President

Figure 32
Gesture signifying leadership.

Saddam Hussain in Baghdad bear witness to this gesture, which in essence is an attempt to embrace the masses.

Included in this general framework of openness, transparency and the open palm are the two practices of handshaking and political proclamation. Proclamation, which is essentially a form of popular support once the leader assumes power, is done by handshaking. In the same vein, any agreement or accord – commercial, political or otherwise – between two people is often sealed by clapping open palms.

Of the other desirable qualities which are expressed by the act of 'highness' are beauty and certainty. Beauty is expressed by joining the thumb to the index finger in a circular shape, leaving the other fingers open, and then raising the hand at the elbow in an acute angle upward towards the face.

Figure 33
Gesture signifying beauty.

This gesture is often accompanied by a slow, simple smile to emphasize the element of confidence, and slightly raising the eyebrows to underline wonder (*figure 33*). Wonder is a way of recognizing beauty.

In expressing ugliness, on the other hand, these gestures are reversed – namely, the fingers assume a questioning position instead of wonder; this is done by opening all the fingers and turning them anti-clockwise as if one deliberately wants to create suspicion. This gesture is often accompanied by slightly moving the mouth sideways with tightened lips raised upward towards the nose (*figure 34*).

Figure 34
Gesture signifying ugliness.

It is possible to use the same gesture signifying beauty to stand for certainty, with some modification, in the movement of the hand. Instead of raising the hand upward towards the head, you move it repeatedly back and forth in a horizontal fashion. Repetition is significant because it stresses the elements of firmness and determination. We say of a hardworking person that he 'grinds' and 'pounds' the object of his interest, meaning he kept on working at it until he made it – a clear reference to repetition.

CHAPTER 13

A Viewpoint for Discussion

While researching and writing this book, I was stunned by the lack of debate on sexual matters in Christianity as opposed to the openness and unreserved discussions in Islam. This lack of debate in Christianity is best shown in the life history of Jesus Christ as narrated in the four Gospels of Matthew, Mark, Luke, and John. In these Gospels there is plenty about Jesus's birth, life, sayings, deeds, miracles, crucifixion, and then his ascendancy to heaven. Although most Christian churches believe that Christ had two natures, divine and human, none of the Gospels deals with his sexual life as a human being. The human side was totally ignored. He did not fall in love, did not marry and failed to practice the sexual life expected of humans. It is perhaps because of this that Christianity considered sheer desire of women an adulterous act. It is cited in Matthew:[1]

> If a man looks at a woman with a lustful eye, he has already committed adultery with her in his heart.

Of course, the lack of debate must not be construed to mean that Christianity failed to deal with other subjects relating to sex; there is plenty on marriage and adultery. The

Gospels speak very strongly of marriage as a sacrament uniting husband and wife in one body. With the exception of sexual life, many recommendations and directives that deal with husband-wife relationships are discussed in some detail.

It is possible to trace the lack of concern with sex to the very definition of the body as divine, which raised it to a state of existence higher than sex, beyond sex. In fact, body divinity and sex are placed on opposite poles. In his First Letter John affirms:

> Do not set your hearts on the godless world or anything in it. Anyone who loves the world is a stranger to the Father's love. Everything the world affords, all that panders to the appetites or entices the eyes, all the glamour of its life, springs not from the Father but from the godless world.[2]

No doubt, the two phrases 'panders to the appetites' and 'entices the eyes' refer, among other things, to sexual life. This means that worldly matters, including sex, and the kingdom of God are irreconcilable demands. If this is so, no wonder then that Christ was born to a virgin impregnated by the Holy Spirit.

The lack of concern with sexual life has prompted Christians in the west to introduce sex education as a required course of study in schools. In this respect, school seems to be replacing the family whose ties are becoming looser in the face of ever-growing technological change. Sex education includes men's and women's physiology – conception, birth, menstruation, stimulation – as well as marriage expectations and relationships, child-rearing practices and the maintenance of an acceptable standard of family life. These matters are added to the school curricula because they are thought to be an integral part of health education.

By comparison, Muslim scholars have been dealing with the ingredients of what is called sex education since the inception of their religion. There are four closely interlinked reasons that explain this concern: (1) the comprehensive nature of Islam, (2) the emphasis placed on *shari'a* in religion, (3) the incorporation of history and traditions into the fabric of religion and (4) the definition of the body as a source of shame and a fountain of impurities.

Muslims interpret the Qur'anic verse, 'The religion before God is Islam'[3] to mean that Islam covers every single aspect of life – worship, marriage, divorce, sex, work, politics, eating, drinking and fasting. The word 'Islam' in this context means obedience to God's will and law as exemplified in the *shari'a*. Unlike Christ who did not live long enough to witness the rise of a Christian state that would legislate for its dogma – Christ started to preach the new faith at thirty and was crucified at thirty three – the Prophet Muhammad preached the new faith, fought its enemies, defeated them and built up the foundation of the Islamic state. He lived his sixty two years of life as a man to the full.

Following the Qur'anic verse, 'The government is none but God,'[4] which is repeated in *sura* 12:40 and in *sura* 12:67, jurists have always striven to translate dogma, as revealed in the Qur'anic texts and practised by the Prophet and his righteous companions, into *shari'a*. Thus, the Prophet's and the companions' life histories, behaviour, actions, sayings, and every aspect of their lives including marriage, divorce and sexual life, assumed a special importance as a basis for religious legislation. Their ways, manners and modes set legal precedents for the forthcoming generations. As a matter of fact, schisms in Islamic history focus precisely on controversies over the traditions Muslims should follow and the companions they should revere and trust.[5]

This means that the Prophet's marriages and his sexual life are meant to set the legal limits for marriage and sex in Islam. Besides, the state of the body and sexual life are not simply physiological matters; they interfere with worship, and therefore, with salvation and the Day of Judgment. The body is full of pollutants that should be purified before approaching God.

Of course, I understand the reasons for Muslims' concern with sexual life, but still the openness and the frankness with which sex issues are dealt is striking. Two things impressed me: firstly, the free and open discussion of the Prophet's sexual life in considerable detail; secondly, the free discussion of various topics pertaining to sex. The first is impressive because the discussion of such topics in public is normally avoided. According to many Muslims, these are moral issues that must be dealt with confidentially in private, within the family walls or between a believer and a well-trained jurist. But, to resort to the *shari'a* and deal with these otherwise normally forbidden issues is permissible, which makes it clear that a researcher who works from within the *shari'a* acquires a great measure of freedom. Let me illustrate this point further.

If al-Sawwaf's book, *Marriage Life According to the Islamic Shari'a* (1995), had been written from the viewpoint of modern social or psychological sciences, it would have been rejected on the spot for its sexual absurdities. On the contrary, it is accepted, cherished and widely read – the copy I bought in Damascus was the fifth edition within one year of its publication. Not only that, but it was prefaced by a lengthy introduction written by Shaikh Ahmad Kaftaru, the *qadi* of the Syrian Republic, the highest position in the religious hierarchy. When some friends and colleagues read at random selected passages from this book they were equally surprised. One commented, 'I would have been put in prison for saying these things.'

The freedom one acquires in dealing with topics pertaining to Islamic *shari'a* raises two general and broader points: (1) the choice of topic and (2) the freedom of research, writing and expression. Because of the comprehensive definition of religion, any topic could be qualified as Islamic – banks, interest rates, medicine, the atomic bomb (as it was paraded as 'The Islamic Bomb' during the army marches in Pakistan in 1998), schools, universities and republics.

The second point raises the question of freedom in general, including political freedom to oppose governments and hold them accountable. Apparently, should this opposition be based on the Islamic *shari'a*, it would be socially accepted and popularly tolerated. No wonder that the bulk of opposition movements in Islam, starting from the Shi'a rebellion in the first year after Muhammad's death to the various Islamic political parties today, are religious. To draw upon religious sources is to acquire a sort of legitimacy for a free political platform. The political agenda of opposition parties in many Arab states today focuses on religious matters. The assumption being: once you please God other things – better economy, finance, education, health, transportation, agriculture, industry – will automatically accrue. If this is so does it mean then that political modernization – democracy, accountability, an open political system, would have to emerge via the Islamic *shari'a*? The issue is open for discussion.

The Traits of Human Language[1]

I. Traits shared between man, mammals, reptiles and insects
   1. The use of the visual-auditory channel
   2. Rapid fading of sounds
   3. Broadcasting in all directions
   4. Interchangeability: the speaker becomes the auditor
   5. Total feedback: the speaker is simultaneously the auditor

II. Traits shared with apes
   6. Specialization: sound clusters are associated with specific referents
   7. The relationship between sound and referent is situationally fixed
   8. The relationship is arbitrary

III. Traits shared with the hominids
   9. Meanings are composed of discrete clusters of sounds
   10. Meanings are transmitted from one generation to another through deliberate instructions

IV. Traits peculiar to man

    11. The capacity to produce new sounds and therefore new meanings

    12. The ability to arrange sound clusters to form new words

    13. The meanings thus produced are non-situational, abstract meanings that go beyond time and place

NOTES

For full publishing details of the works mentioned, the reader is referred to the bibliography.

Preface
1. *Sura* 49:12. In this book the number of the *sura* in the Qur'an precedes the number of the verse. Thus 49:12 means *sura* 49, verse 12. For the English translation of Qur'anic verses, I have consulted with 'Abdallah Yusuf 'Ali's translation.

Chapter 1
1. *Sura* 4:3.
2. *Sura* 4:34.
3. In fact, social divisions are derived from body divisions as demonstrated in Pandolfo's work on a Moroccan village (see Bibliography).
4. Khuri, 1993, p. 91.
5. *Sura* 3:4.

Chapter 2
1. Ibn Manzur, p. 458.
2. *Sura* 16:2.
3. *Sura* 70:4.
4. *Sura* 15:29.
5. *Sura* 21:91.
6. Genesis 2:7. All biblical references are taken from The New English Bible, United Kingdom: Oxford and Cambridge University Presses, 1970.

7. *Sura* 23:12.
8. Communion is the holy, sacramental partaking made of a mixture of wine, bread and warm water which symbolically stand for Christ's body, blood and flesh. The consumption of the body of Christ transforms the congregation from a mundane status to a divine one.
9. *Sura* 2:222.
10. *Sura* 5:7.
11. *Sura* 8:11.
12. *Sura* 3:42.
13. *Sura* 3:55.
14. *Sura* 9:103.
15. *Sura* 9:28.
16. *Al-azlam* and *al-ansab*, which recur in this verse, refer to different types of divinatory techniques.
17. *Sura* 6:145.
18. *Sura* 9:125.
19. *Sura* 6:125.
20. See *suras* 2:59; 7:134; 7:135; 8:11; 29:34; 34:5; and 45:11.
21. Ibn Manzur, p. 112.
22. *Sura* 25:48.
23. For more details, see Maghniyah, pp. 10–25.
24. Bandali, pp. 21–66.
25. Concerning rites of passage, see Van Gennep's work.

Chapter 3

1. Antoun, pp. 671–97.
2. *Sura* 24:30.
3. *Sura* 24:31.
4. *Sura* 33:35.
5. Ibn Manzur, pp. 1065–7.
6. *Suras* 24:30–31; 70:29; 21:91; and 66:12.
7. Ibn Manzur, p. 1066.
8. For details, see Dolgin, Kemintzer and Shneider, pp. 1–47.
9. *Sura* 24:31.
10. *Sura* 24:58.

11. *Sura* 33:32.
12. *Sura* 33:35.
13. *Sura* 4:1.
14. *Sura* 3:14.
15. *Sura* 4:43.
16. See the book on *The Teaching of Prayer and Ablution According to the Hanafi School of Law*, n. d., p. 22; see also Maghniyah, vol. 1, p. 152.
17. Ware, p. 42.
18. Luke 3:6.
19. Ware, p. 74.
20. Genesis 1:26–27.
21. Vaporis, p. 44.
22. Ware, pp. 219–24.
23. Ibid., pp. 224–6.
24. *Sura* 7:11.
25. *Sura* 64:3.
26. Psalm 82:6–7.
27. John 10:34.
28. 1 Cor 6:13.
29. 1 Cor 6:18.
30. 1 Cor 6:19–20.
31. 1 Cor 6:16.
32. 1 Cor 7:14.
33. John 6:48–58.
34. For details, see Msirra, pp. 8–11.
35. 1 Cor 6:15.
36. See *Bibliography*.

Chapter 4
1. 10:9–16.
2. 14:14–17.
3. Mark 7:18–23.
4. Luke 4:36; 6:18; and 11:24.
5. Matthew 5:17.

6. *Sura* 6:146.
7. Maghniyah, p. 370.
8. *Sura* 7:157.
9. Maghniyah, pp. 371–2.
10. Leviticus 11:9–12.
11. Maghniyah, p. 374.
12. *Sura* 6:145.
13. Maghniyah, pp. 370–1.
14. Ibid., p. 371.
15. See Fiennes.
16. Ibn Kathir, vol. 4, pp. 9–11.
17. These are various ways in which an animal might be killed.
18. Douglas, p. 55.
19. For details, see the Book of Genesis, Old Testament.
20. Douglas, p. 55.
21. See Claude Levi-Strauss for more details on the concept of binary opposition.
22. This medical information was cited in *Time* magazine, 15 January 1996, pp. 42–3.
23. *Sura* 112:1–4.
24. *Sura* 49:10.
25. *Sura* 61:4.
26. Ibn Kathir, p. 359.
27. Leviticus 15:6; 12:1; Maghniyah, vol. 1, p. 376; and *Teaching the Style of Prayer and Ablution According to the Hanafi School*, pp. 6–8.

Chapter 5

1. Turner, p. 188.
2. *Sura* 7:130.
3. Mussa, pp. 73–7.
4. Ibid., p. 79.
5. Maghniyah, vol. 1, p. 91; Mussa, p. 89.
6. Leviticus 12:4.
7. Ibid., 15:19–20.

8. From the minutes of the Antiochian Church's Holy Synod held on 28 May 1997.
9. See Muhammad Hussain Fadlallah's article in *al-Nahar* daily, 12 October 1995.
10. Ibn Manzur, vol. 1, p. 1017.
11. 2:17.
12. 19: 34.
13. 26: 28.
14. Genesis:22:9–14.
15. 9:6.

Chapter 6
1. *Sura* 5:7.
2. *Sura* 18:46.
3. *Sura* 57:20.
4. *Sura* 3:14.
5. *Suras* 8:28; 9:69; 17:6, 17:64; 26:133; 34:35; 57:20; 63:9; and 68:14.
6. *Sura* 63:9.
7. *Sura* 102:1–2.
8. Mhanna, p. 69.
9. Ibid.
10. Knaifani, p. 41.
11. al-Sawwaf, p. 132.
12. al-Sawwaf, p. 16.
13. Ibid., p. 17.
14. Ibid., p. 17.
15. Sa'd al-Din, p. 18.
16. *Sura* 22:5.
17. Mussa, p. 52.
18. *Sura* 2:223.
19. al-Sayyuti, p. 47.
20. al-Sawwaf, p. 128.
21. Yahfufi, pp. 170–3.
22. *Sura* 2:222.

23. Ibn Kathir, vol. 1, pp. 260–5.
24. Yahfufi, pp. 159–64.
25. Ibn Kathir, vol. 1, p. 259.
26. al-Sawwaf, p. 15.
27. Yahfufi, p. 9.
28. Ibid., p. 149.
29. Ibid., pp. 7–8.
30. Mhanna, p. 69.
31. Sa'd al-Din, p. 35.
32. *Sura* 36:55–56.
33. *Sura* 56:35–37.
34. *Sura* 56:22–23.
35. *Sura* 30:21.
36. *Sura* 2:187.
37. Rida, p. 16.
38. *Sura* 2:187.
39. Harun, pp. 264–5.
40. There is no scientific basis that justifies this belief. Some believe the contrary is true.
41. al-Sawwaf, p. 117.
42. This is taken from *Sahih Muslim*, No. 56, p. 223.
43. al-Sawwaf, pp. 114–5.
44. Ibid., pp. 114–5.
45. Ibn al-Athir, p. 744.
46. Harun, pp. 264–5.
47. For more details, see al-Sawwaf, p. 83.
48. al-Sawwaf, p. 107.
49. Ibid., p. 132.
50. Abi Dawud, p. 79.
51. al-Albani, p. 148.
52. al-Sawwaf, p. 134.
53. Ibid., p. 134.
54. For more details, see al-Sawwaf, pp. 133–4.
55. al-Sawwaf, p. 109.
56. Ibid., p. 134.

57. Ibid., p. 112.
58. Maghniyah, vol. 1, p. 8.
59. Knaifani, p. 29.
60. Ibid., p. 16.
61. Ibid., p. 16.
62. Maghniyah, vol. 1, pp. 80–5.
63. Ibid., p. 80.
64. Yahfufi, pp. 73–4.
65. Ibid., pp. 73–4.

Chapter 7
1. See Hockett.
2. See Schaller.
3. Deans, pp. 19–21.
4. For more details, see Birdwhistell, and Mehralian.
5. *Sura* 48:10.
6. Morris, p. 155.
7. Pease, pp. 107–9.

Chapter 8
1. Pease, p. 21.
2. Fallers, pp. 243–60.
3. See Bu Shrara.
4. Following a conversation with Dr Latif Abul-Husn in Spring 1999.
5. For details, see Pease, pp. 20–1.

Chapter 9
1. Ibn Kathir, vol. 4, p. 325.
2. *Sura* 20:5.
3. *Sura* 85:11.
4. *Sura* 2:256.
5. Khuri, 1968.

Chapter 10
1. Khuri, 1993, p. 28.
2. *Sura* 24:24.
3. Morris, pp. 76–7.
4. After a discussion with Dr Paul Sa'd in Winter 1999.
5. *Sura* 24:31.
6. Ibn Kathir, vol. 3, p. 285.
7. The 'V' sign is taken from the word victory in English.

Chapter 11
1. 'Atwi, p. 140.
2. Genesis, Chapter 3.
3. *Sura* 20:120–121.
4. *Sura* 20:122–123.
5. *Sura* 30:21.
6. *Sura* 56:35–38.
7. Khuri, 1975, p. 140.
8. al-Sayyuti, p. 711.
9. Ibn Manzur, vol. 1, p. 315.
10. al-Tabarani, pp. 140–2.
11. al-Sawwaf, pp. 64–86.
12. *Sura* 4:19.
13. *Sura* 2:228.
14. *Sura* 4:34.
15. Qabbani, 1993, a, p. 124.
16. Ibid., p. 136.
17. Ibid., p. 138.
18. Ibid., p. 140.
19. Ibid., p. 142.
20. Ibid., p. 170.
21. Qabbani, 1993, b, p. 15.
22. Qabbani, 1983, a, p. 37.
23. Ibid., p. 64.
24. Ibid.
25. Ibid., p. 289.

26. Ibid., p. 332.
27. Ibid., p. 376.
28. After a conversation with Mulla 'Isa in 1975.

Chapter 12
1. *Sura* 21:20.

Chapter 13
1. 5: 28.
2. First Letter of John 2:15–16.
3. *Sura* 3:19.
4. *Sura* 6:57.
5. Khuri, 1990, p. 3.

Appendix
1. The data is taken from a lecture given by the late professor Theodore Stern at the University of Oregon in 1962.

BIBLIOGRAPHY

English

Antoun, Richard. 'On the Modesty of Women in Arab Muslim Villages', *American Anthropologist*, 70: 671–97, 1968.

Birdwhistell, R. L. *Kinestics and Context*, Louisville (Kentucky): University of Louisville Press, 1971.

Cohen, David. *Body Language in Relationships*, London: Sheldon Press, 1995.

Darwin, C. *The Expression of Emotion in Man and Animals*, New York, Applaton-Century Crafts, 1872.

Deans, Alexander. *Bees and Beekeeping*, London: Oliver and Boyd Ltd, 1962.

Dolgin, L. Janet, David S. Kemintzker, and David M. Shneider (eds). 'As People Express their Lives, So They Are', *Symbolic Anthropology*, New York: Columbia University Press, 1977.

Douglas, Mary. *Purity and Danger*, London: Routledge, 1966.

Fallers, L. and Margaret Fallers. 'Sex Roles in Edremit', *Mediterranean Family Structures*, J. C. Peristiany (ed.), Cambridge: Cambridge University Press.

Fiennes, R. N. *Zoonoses and the Origins and Ecology of Human Disease*, London: Academic Press, 1978.

Gennep, Van. *Les rites de passage*, translated into English by M. Vizedom and G. I. Coffee, Chicago: Chicago University Press, 1960.

Hockett, F. C. *A Course in Modern Linguistics*, New York: The Macmillan Company, 1958.

Khuri, Fuad I. 'The Etiquette of Bargaining in the Middle East', *American Anthropologist*, 70: 698–706, 1968.

—— *From Village to Suburb*, Chicago: Chicago University Press, 1975.

—— *Tribe and State in Bahrain*, Chicago: Chicago University Press, 1980.

—— *Imams and Emirs: State, Religion, and Sect in Islam*. London: Saqi Books, 1990.

Levi-Strauss, Claude. *The Raw and the Cooked*, New York: Harper and Row, 1969.

Mehralian, A. *A Silent Language*, Belmont (California): Nordworth, 1971.

Morris, D. Bodytalk: *A Good Guide to Gestures*, London: Jonathan Cape, 1994.

Pease, A. *Body Language*, London: Sheldon Press, 1981.

Pondolfo, Stephina. 'Detours of Life: Space and Bodies in a Moroccan Village', *American Anthropologist*, 16: 3–23, 1989.

Schaller, G. B. *The Mountain Gorilla: Ecology and Behaviour*, Chicago: Chicago University Press, 1963.

Smith, W. Robertson. *Lectures on the Religion of the Semites*, New York: Meridian Books, 1957.

Turner, Victor W., 'Symbols in African Ritual', *Symbolic Anthropology*, Janet Dolgin, David Kemintzer, and David Shneider (eds), New York: Columbia University Press, 1977.

Vaporis, N. Michael, (ed.). *Daily Prayers for Orthodox Christians*, Brookline: Holy Cross Orthodox Press, 1986.

Ware, Timothy. *The Orthodox Church*, Great Britain: The Chaucer Press Ltd., 1963.

Arabic

'Abd al-Baqi, Muhammad Fuad. *al-Mu'jam al-Mufahras li alfaz al-Qur'an al-Karim* (The Indexed Concordance for the Lexicons of the Generous Qur'an), Beirut: Dar al-Ma'rifa, 1991.

Abi Dawud, Sulaiman. *Sunnan Abi Dawud* (The Directives of

Abi Dawud), Ahmad Muhammad Shakir and Muhammad Hamid al-Faqi (eds), Beirut: Dar al-Ma'rifa, 1980.

Al-Albani, Muhammad Nassir al-Din. *Sunnan Ibn Maja* (The Directives of Ibn Maja), Beirut: al-Maktab al-Islami, 1988.

Ali, Abdallah Y. *al-Qur'an al-Karim* (The Generous Qur'an), Beirut: Dar al-'Arabiyah, n. d.

'Atwi, Fawzi (ed.). *Sharh al-Mu'allaqat al-'Ashr* (The Explanation of the Ten Epics), Beirut: al-Sharika al-Lubnaniyah lil-Kitab,1969.

Bandali, Costi. *Madkhal Ila al-Quddas al-Ilahi* (An Introduction to the Holy Liturgy), Beirut: al-Nur Publications, 1961.

Bu Shrara, Traki. *Amkinat al-Jasad fi al-Islam* (The Places of the Body in Islam), translated by Zaina Kafruni, Kuwait: Dar Su'ad al-Sabbah, 1996.

Harun, 'Abd al-Salam Muhammad. *al-Alf al-Mukhtara min Sahih al-Bukhari* (The One Thousand Selected and Authenticated Hadiths of al-Bukhari), Beirut: Dar al-Mallah, 1979.

Ibn al-Athir, Majd al-Din. *Jami' al-Usul fi ahadith al-Rassul* (Concordance of the Authentic Prophet's Sayings), vol. 4, Abdul-Qadir al-Arna'ut (ed.), Beirut: Dar al-Mallah, 1970.

Ibn Kathir, al-Hafiz 'Imad al-Din. *Tafsir al-Qur'an al-'Azim* (The Interpretation of the Great Qur'an), vols. 3 and 4, Beirut: Dar al-Ma'rifa, 1983.

Ibn Manzur Jamal al-Din Abul-Fadl. *Lisan al-'Arab* (the Arab Tongue), vols. 1 and 2, Beirut: Dar Lisan al-'Arab, n. d.

Khuri, F. I. *al-Dhuhniya al-'Arabiya* (The Arab Mentality), Beirut: Dar al-Saqi, 1993.

Knaifani, Jamal al-Din. *al-'Ada al-Sirriya baina al-Tub wal-Islam* (Masturbation Between Medicine and Islam), Beirut: Dar al-Mujtama' al-Islami, n. d.

Maghniyah, Muhammad Jawad. *Fiqh al-Imam Ja'far al-Sadiq* (The Jurisdiction of Imam Ja'far al-Sadiq), vol. 4, Beirut: Dar al-'Ilm lil-Malayyin, 1965.

Mhanna, Jarasimus. *Rasa'il al-Jahiz* (The Letters of al-Jahiz), Beirut: n. p., 1925.

Muslim, Abi al-Hassan. *Sahih Muslim* (The Authentic Hadiths of *Sahih Muslim*), vol. 1, Beirut: Dar al-Fikr, 1978.

Mussa, Kamil. *al-Haid wa Ahkamihi al-Shar'iya* (Menstruation and its Legal Rules), Beirut: Mu'assasat al-Risala, 1983.

n. a. *Ta'lim al-wudu' wa al-salat 'ala al-madhhab al-hanafi* (The Teaching of Prayer and Ablution According to the Hanafi School of Law), No place of publishing, n. p., n. d.

Qabbani, Nizqr. *al-A'mal al-Shi'riya al-Kamila* (The Complete Works of Poetry), vol. 2, Beirut: Nizar Qabbani Publications, 1983.

—— *al-A'mal al-Shi'riya al-Kamila* (The Complete Works of Poetry), vols. 4 and 5, Beirut: Nizar Qabbani Publications, 1993.

Rida, Muhammad Rashid. *Nida' lil-Jins al-Latif fi Huquq al-Nisa' fil-Islam* (A Call for the Opposite Sex Concerning the Rights of Women in Islam), Cairo: Matba'at al-Manar, 1351 h.

Sa'd al-Din, Laila. *al-Mar'at fil-Islam* (The Woman in Islam), Amman: Maktabat al-Risala al-Haditha, 1980.

Sa'ib, Hassan. *Islam al-Hurriya la Islam al-'Ubudiya* (Freedom Islam not Slavery Islam), Beirut: Dar al-'Ilm lil-Malayyin, 1979.

—— *al-Islam wa Tahaddiyat al-'Asr* (Islam and the Challenges of Modern Times), Beirut: Dar al-'Ilm lil-Malayyin, 1981.

al-Sawwaf, Muhammad Sharif. *al-Hayat al-Zawjiyah min Minzar al-Shari'a al-Islamiyah* (Married Life According to Islamic *Shari'a*), Damascus: Dar al-Sanabil, 1994.

al-Sayyuti, Jalal al-Din. *Tafsir al-Jalalain* (The Interpretation of the Qur'an), Beirut: Maktabat al-'Ulum al-Diniyah, 1979.

al-Tabarani, Ibn Ahmad Sulaiman. *Al-Mu'jam al-kabir* (The Great Concordance), Beirut: Maktabat al-Taw'iyah al-Islamiyah, 1980.

Yahfufi, Sulaiman. *Daman al-Jins fil-Islam* (The Insurance of Sex in Islam), Beirut: al-Dar al-'Alamiyah, 1984.

INDEX